Amazing World Records of Language and Literature

Sunflower
education
Exceptional Books for Teachers and Parents

A Great Way to Teach Language and Literature!

Capture students' imagination with a jaw-dropping world record and then build on that interest to teach core ideas. For example, the record-setter for the Language with the Most Words (it's actually English) leads students into a deeper understanding of affixes and appreciation of the work of lexicographers. The World's Oldest Propaganda (hint: it's political) has students identifying types of propaganda and becoming aware of their community. Students read cuneiform, write poetry, outline a screenplay, and even stage a race in a library. A wonderful variety of activities that both deepen and broaden students' knowledge of language and literature.

Grades 5-9. Aligned with the NCTE/IRA Standards

60 Reproducible Activity Sheets • Teaching Tips • Complete Answer Key

Part of the Amazing World Records Series of books!

WorldRecordsBooks.com

Please feel free to photocopy the activity sheets in this book within reason. Sunflower Education grants teachers permission to photocopy the activity sheets from this book for educational use. This permission is granted to individual teachers and not entire schools or school systems. For information or questions regarding permissions, please send an email to permissions@SunflowerEducation.net.

Visit **SunflowerEducation.Net** for more great books!

Editorial   Sunflower Education

Design   Cynthia Hannon Design

Photography
Cover and title page images: © iStockphoto LP.
Interior images: © Wikimedia Commons

ISBN-13: 978-1-937166-03-8
ISBN-10: 1-937166-03-1
Copyright © 2013
Sunflower Education
All rights reserved.
Printed in the U.S.A.

Contents

WORLD RECORDS OF LITERATURE

To the Teacher

Amazing World Records of Language and Literature welcomes students to the superlatives of language and literature. In these pages, they—and you—will learn about some of the most remarkable words and works ever created.

Amazing World Records of Language and Literature is one in a series of books that explores the superlatives of a variety of subjects. Other titles in the series include *Amazing World Records of Geography, Amazing World Records of History, Amazing World Records of Weather,* and *Amazing World Records of Science and Technology.*

Topic Coverage

This is an eclectic collection. Topic range from the world's first language to the world's most controversial book. There are scores of "world records" in language and literature. This collection is an attempt to gather those that are particularly interesting to students, useful as gateways to discussion of standard concepts, germane to general student learning, and of high general pedagogical value.

How this Book is Organized

Amazing World Records of Language and Literature is a supplementary book, conceived and designed for you to utilize at your discretion. However, it is possible to use the book as a stand-alone text to introduce students to dozens of major ideas in language and literature. The book is organized to make both options viable. If you choose the book as a text, guide students through it progressively.

Units

The world records are organized into two general units: World Records of Language and World Records of Literature. Each unit includes two to six chapters.

Chapters

Each chapter addresses a particular world record. Each chapter opens with a teacher's page that provides objectives, teaching tips, and extension and enrichment activities. Each chapter includes three reproducible student activity sheets.

Student Activity Sheets

The first activity sheet always introduces the world record. The following two activity sheets vary in format, content, and student activity. In general, they expand on the record-setting feature to introduce students to qualities of the feature.

How to Use This Book

The student activity sheets are at the heart of *Amazing World Records of Language and Literature*. Virtually all of them can be used as the basis for individual, partner, group, or whole-class activities. They are designed to be extremely flexible. They are self-explanatory. Your judgment is the central guide for how to best use them in your classroom. For further instruction, consult the information presented on the Teacher Guide Page.

Some Final Thoughts

However you integrate *Amazing World Records of Language and Literature* into your classroom, always keep in mind that the student activity sheets provide countless opportunities to foster broader and deeper awareness of the power of words. Keep in mind, too, that students learn best when they're having fun. Foster surprise, delight, and awe, about these superlatives of human communication. Emphasize the drama that underlies every world record of language and literature. Do your best to evoke wonderment of human expression.

NCTE/IRA Standards

1. Students read a wide range of print and non-print texts to build an understanding of texts, of themselves, and of the cultures of the United States and the world; to acquire new information; to respond to the needs and demands of society and the workplace; and for personal fulfillment. Among these texts are fiction and nonfiction, classic and contemporary works.

2. Students read a wide range of literature from many periods in many genres to build an understanding of the many dimensions (e.g., philosophical, ethical, aesthetic) of human experience.

3. Students apply a wide range of strategies to comprehend, interpret, evaluate, and appreciate texts. They draw on their prior experience, their interactions with other readers and writers, their knowledge of word meaning and of other texts, their word identification strategies, and their understanding of textual features (e.g., sound-letter correspondence, sentence structure, context, graphics).

4. Students adjust their use of spoken, written, and visual language (e.g., conventions, style, vocabulary) to communicate effectively with a variety of audiences and for different purposes.

5. Students employ a wide range of strategies as they write and use different writing process elements appropriately to communicate with different audiences for a variety of purposes.

6. Students apply knowledge of language structure, language conventions (e.g., spelling and punctuation), media techniques, figurative language, and genre to create, critique, and discuss print and non-print texts.

7. Students conduct research on issues and interests by generating ideas and questions, and by posing problems. They gather, evaluate, and synthesize data from a variety of sources (e.g., print and non-print texts, artifacts, people) to communicate their discoveries in ways that suit their purpose and audience.

8. Students use a variety of technological and information resources (e.g., libraries, databases, computer networks, video) to gather and synthesize information and to create and communicate knowledge.

9. Students develop an understanding of and respect for diversity in language use, patterns, and dialects across cultures, ethnic groups, geographic regions, and social roles.

10. Students whose first language is not English make use of their first language to develop competency in the English language arts and to develop understanding of content across the curriculum.

11. Students participate as knowledgeable, reflective, creative, and critical members of a variety of literacy communities.

12. Students use spoken, written, and visual language to accomplish their own purposes (e.g., for learning, enjoyment, persuasion, and the exchange of information).

World Records of Language

1. The World's First Language

Sign Language

NCTE/IRA Standards
• 4, 9, 12

Time Required
• About two class periods

Teaching Tips

Students may work on the activity sheets individually, with a partner, or with a small group.

Activity Sheet 1A
• Emphasize that language predates writing and leaves no fossils.
• Remind students of the connection between the terms *prehistoric* and *historic* as they relate to written records.

Activity Sheet 1B
• Encourage students to be creative as they invent signs.
• Emphasize the theoretical evolution of language from iconic signs to more advanced forms.

Activity Sheet 1C
• Encourage students to brainstorm the different environments and times in which vocal and sign languages may be more advantageous.

Answers

• **Activity Sheet 1A** 1. Language developed long before writing did; and hence as far as we know, the first language was not recorded anywhere; 2. writing; 3. Iconic signs allow communication between individuals even if they shared no common language prior to their interaction with each other; 4. Some argue that it is unclear why, if the first language was based on iconic gestures, humans would later switch to verbal languages.

• **Activity Sheet 1B** 1-2. Encourage creativity, but be sure students understand that the objective is to communicate the idea as clearly as possible. Help them notice which signs they create are iconic and which are not. Generally the iconic ones should be easier for others to understand; help students make this connection and relate it back to the theory that sign language was the first language.

• **Activity Sheet 1C** Reward thoughtful responses that take into account realistic scenarios.

Extension and Enrichment

• Can students think of any examples of iconic vocal language? Introduce them to the concept of *onomatopoeia* and discuss whether the potential for vocal language to be iconic should be seen as a threat to the theory that sign language developed first.
• Students can conduct research and postulate theories about early language. Do they agree that sign language probably developed first? Supposing that it did, how do they think it might have evolved into a spoken language? Students can study sign language to better understand the use of iconic gestures.

Visit WorldRecordsBooks.com for more images and activities!

Name _____ Class _____ Date _____

Directions: Read the article and complete the activities.

We can never know for sure when the first language developed, who made it, or what it was like.

The only conclusive, lasting evidence we have of language is writing, and language existed for a very long time before the development of writing.

Language is a remarkably powerful invention. It is hard to imagine how humans could have developed a world with airplanes, medicine, or even farming without it. Language even shapes many of our thoughts.

One of the world's great mysteries is how language began. Scientists have lots of theories about the first language. One idea is that it was a sign language. Unlike most elements in a vocal language, signs in sign language can be *iconic,* which means that they resemble the thing they represent. Because of this resemblance, an iconic gesture can make us think of the object it stands for, even if we never have seen the gesture before and no one explains its meaning to us. For example, flapping your arms can represent a bird. Because they are easy to understand, iconic gestures might allow communication between individuals who do not otherwise share a common language.

One possible objection to the theory that signs were used before speech is that it is unclear why, if humans already knew a language of gestures, they would later switch to a language of sounds.

1. The author of the article writes, "We can never know for sure when the first language developed, who made it, or what it was like." Why is this true?

   _____

   _____

   _____

2. What is the only indisputable, lasting proof of language?

   _____

   _____

3. Why does it make sense that the world's first language might have been a sign language?

_____

_____

_____

_____

_____

4. What is an objection to this theory?

_____

_____

_____

_____

_____

_____

"A-S-L" signed with American Sign Language

Name _____ Class _____ Date _____

Directions: After your teacher divides you into small groups, come up with a gesture to communicate each of the words below. Be imaginative. After you have come up with a gesture for each word, select a few that you think best communicate the intended meanings and present them to the class.

Meaning	Sketch of Sign
water	
rain	
book	
computer	
flying	
swimming	
reading	
tree	
sun	
green	
belief	
dream	

Were your classmates able to understand which words your signs represented? The last few words were probably the hardest to convey because they are *intangible,* which means that you can't physically touch them. This activity should help you think about the challenge which early humans faced as they began to develop the first language. They had to deal with many more concepts than are found in the twelve words listed here, though.

Now try the same activity, but this time come up with a vocal sound rather than a gesture for each concept. Avoid using words from any language you know. After you are done, think about what happened and answer the following questions.

1. Which time did you communicate the meaning of the words more clearly to your classmates?

_____

_____

_____

_____

2. Was it easier to come up with an iconic gesture or an iconic sound? Why do you think this is the case?

_____

_____

_____

_____

_____

_____

_____

_____

_____

Name _____ Class _____ Date _____

We don't know what the first language was like, and, barring time travel, we may never know for certain. However, we do understand some aspects of what life was like for early people. Language of any form would have been very beneficial. Using the information we have, we can theorize about what the likely benefits of sign language or vocal language would have been.

Directions: Consider the lives of early people. Their daily activities revolved around surviving. Here are some of their probable tasks: gathering food; building shelters; creating tools, clothing, and weapons; hunting; fishing; and avoiding predators. What would the advantages of sign language be for someone in this situation? What would be the advantages of vocal language?

Advantages of Sign Language	Advantages of Vocal Language

2. The World's Most Widespread Language Family
Indo-European

NCTE/IRA Standards
• 4, 7, 8, 9, 11, 12

Time Required
• About two class periods

Teaching Tips
Students may work on the activity sheets individually, with a partner, or with a small group.

Activity Sheet 2A
• Emphasize the strong connection between languages in the same language family.
• Help students accurately understand the ways in which languages are like family members.

Activity Sheet 2B
• Take this opportunity to explain how to find and understand the history of a word using the dictionary. If students do use dictionaries for their research, encourage them to use other sources as well. You may want to assign them a question about their words which cannot be answered using the dictionary alone.
• Remind students that they encounter borrowed words daily.
• Work with students on their presentation skills before having them present to the entire class.

Activity Sheet 2C
• Remind students that connections between words from different languages can be subtle.
• Lead a class discussion using the questions as guidelines. Help students realize that some language families are much larger than others and that there can be language families within language families.
• Encourage multilingual students to bring up connections they have noticed between words in their different languages.

Answers
• *Activity Sheet 2A* 1. A group of similar languages that developed from the same source; the Indo-European language family; 2. Answers should include a word that originated in another language; 3. Romance, Indo-Iranian, Germanic, Slavic, Baltic, Greek, and Celtic languages; 4. A language is dead if no one speaks it as a primary language. A language is extinct if it is not spoken at all; 5. Vocabulary, grammar, and pronunciation.
• *Activity Sheet 2B* Reward thoughtful, well-researched presentations.
• *Activity Sheet 2C* Sino-Tibetan: muk (Chinese), mig (Tibetan), mjak (Burmese), mit (Lushai) Semitic: ayin (Hebrew), ayn (Arabic), yn (Phoenician) Austronesian: taa (Thai) Indo-European: occhio (Italian), súil (Irish Gaelic), ankha (Hindi), auge (German).

Extension and Enrichment
• Have students research borrowed words from non-Indo-European languages.
• In conjunction with a foreign language class, students can compare and contrast the grammar of a foreign language with that of their native tongue.

Visit WorldRecordsBooks.com for more images and activities!

Name _____ Class _____ Date _____

Directions: Read the article and complete the activities.

How alike are you and the members of your family? Even if you and your siblings look and act differently, at the most basic level you are very similar; on average, people who have the same biological parents share about 25% of their genome. Cousins, on the other hand, do not have the same parents and hence are less alike than siblings. Nevertheless, they have one set of grandparents in common and consequently share 6.25% of their genome.

Just like people are descendants of their parents and grandparents, each language comes from a parent language which in turn came from a parent language of its own. These relationships are used to classify languages into *families*. As you might expect, the closer in a family one tongue is to another, the more characteristics they have in common. For example, one language family contains Spanish, Romanian, Italian, French, and Portuguese. These are known as the Romance languages because they all descended from Latin, the language spoken by the Romans. Because they all came from the same language, these are, in a sense, "sister" tongues, and they share more traits with one another than they do with their "aunts" and "cousins."

Just as each of the Romance languages belongs to the same family, even language families are related to one another. The Romance, Indo-Iranian , Germanic , Slavic, Baltic, Greek, and Celtic language families all belong to one very large family called Indo-European. Half of the world speaks an Indo-European language. This makes it the most widespread language family on Earth.

Unlike siblings and cousins, languages split from a single earlier language. Historical linguists examine similarities in different languages' vocabulary, grammar, and pronunciation in order to figure out what their parent language was like. This can be a very difficult task. Languages change over time in unpredictable ways and borrow words from unrelated languages. A *borrowed word* is a word in one language that is adopted by another language. For example, even though Japanese and English derive from different language families, "kimono" is a Japanese word which we now use in modern English. If you were able to keep tracing back up the family trees of all the world's language families, in theory, you should reach the first language. This process gets harder the further back in history you go since the more ancient and obscure the language, the fewer written records there are with which to work.

Rather than focus on deciphering ancient languages, many linguists today are working hard to preserve modern ones. We are living in a time when an unprecedented number of languages are disappearing. Without a record of them, we will forever lose important information which might have helped us learn more about the language families to which these languages belonged.

For example, linguists are recording some of the last Salish speakers in Montana. Salish has been spoken from Montana to Eastern Canada for thousands of years. If it is preserved now, it may die, but it will not become extinct. (Notice that "dead" and "extinct" are each used in a very particular way when referring to languages. If a language is dead, that means that no one speaks it as a main tongue. An extinct language is no longer spoken by anyone at all.)

1. What is a language family? Which language family is the most widespread?

_____

_____

2. What is a borrowed word? Try to think of three new examples.

_____

_____

3. List the groups of languages that make up the world's most widespread language family.

_____

_____

4. What is the difference between a dead language and an extinct language?

_____

_____

_____

5. What aspects of languages do historical linguists look at to determine language families?

_____

_____

Name _____ Class _____ Date _____

Directions: Select one of the three borrowed words you wrote down on Activity Sheet 2A. Conduct research on the origins of your borrowed word and prepare a brief presentation of what you find. Be sure to include important facts such as the word's language of origin, how long ago it was borrowed, and any changes in its meaning, usage, or pronunciation. At the end of your presentation, postulate a theory for why your word was borrowed.

_____

_____

_____

_____

_____

_____

_____

_____

_____

_____

_____

_____

_____

_____

_____

_____

_____

_____

_____

_____

_____

_____

_____

Name _____ Class _____ Date _____

How closely related do you think the languages of the following two quotes are?

"Wæs he se mon in weoruldhade geseted oð þa tide þe he wæs gelyfdre ylde, ond næfre nænig leoð geleornade."

"The man was established in worldly life until the time when he was of advanced age, and he had never learned any songs."

These sentences say the same thing in different versions of the *same* language! The top quote is a line in Old English, and the bottom quote is the modern English translation. (The sentence itself is an excerpt from Bede's *Account of the Poet Caedmon*.) As demonstrated here, languages change so much over time that it can be very difficult to determine how they looked, sounded, and functioned in the past.

Directions: Linguists perform massive amounts of vocabulary checking in order to find similarities between languages. Examine the following words for "eye" closely and try grouping them into language families:

ankha, muk, occhio, ayn, mit, auge, súil, yn, taa, mjak, mig, ayin

Group Discussion: Once you have had time to complete the above exercise, your teacher will share the correct answers with you. As a group, discuss the following questions:

- Which groupings did you get right, and how did you figure out which words to include in them?

- Which groupings surprised you? Can you see any similarities between the words in these groups?

- Why might words in one language family seem to have more in common with one another than words in a different language family?

- Do you know any words from a language other than English? If so, can you see any connection between these words and words with the same or similar meanings in English?

NCTE/IRA Standards
• 8, 12

Time Required
• About two class periods

Teaching Tips
Students may work on the activity sheets individually, with a partner, or with a small group.

Activity Sheet 3A
• Emphasize that living languages constantly change.
• Remind students about borrowed words.

Activity Sheet 3B
• Encourage students to be creative as they come up with synonyms and antonyms.

Activity Sheet 3C
• Encourage students to be concise.
• Remind students that dictionary entries should be clear enough for most people to understand.

Answers
• *Activity Sheet 3A* 1. Languages are constantly changing, and many that may have large vocabularies are not as well documented as English; 2. English; 3. Answers will vary; reward thoughtful responses; 4. Even if lexicographers stopped updating dictionaries, the language would not stop changing. We would wind up with outdated dictionaries that no longer accurately describe our language.
• *Activity Sheet 3B* Encourage creativity, but be sure students correctly select synonyms and antonyms.
• *Activity Sheet 3C* Reward clear and thoughtful responses.

Extension and Enrichment
• Students can research languages of trade and business (such as Indonesian) that have not been as well documented as English.
• Students can create their own dictionary with definitions they find clear.

Visit WorldRecordsBooks.com for more images and activities!

Name _____ Class _____ Date _____

Directions: Read the article and complete the activities.

It is impossible to know for certain which language uses the largest number of words, but many people think that this distinction belongs to the English language.

At the very least, we do know that English has one of the largest vocabularies belonging to a modern, well-documented language. Since it has come to be used as the primary language of trade and business throughout much of the world, it is spoken alongside many diverse tongues, and, consequently many of opportunities to borrow words from them. Over time, these borrowed words become accepted additions to it. One result of acquiring a lot of borrowed words is that English has many *synonyms*—words whose meanings are the same or very similar.

There are several reasons why it is hard to know definitely which language has the most words. For one thing, living languages constantly change. People come up with new words and stop using older ones. Borrowed words are another source of change. The process of adopting foreign words continues in English and other languages to this day. Because languages exist in a constant state of flux, it is difficult to determine at any given time exactly how many words belong to a particular tongue.

Another important reason behind the uncertainty about which language contains the most words is that we do not have enough records of other world languages. English as a language is studied and documented in dictionaries more than many other tongue. Thus, although we know that English has a very large vocabulary, there might be another, less studied language which has an even larger one.

All of that being said, experts estimate that there are *at least* 250,000 English words. (If you include different tenses of words, the number is near 750,000.) More than 50 percent of them are nouns, and about 25 percent of them are adjectives. Verbs make up 15 percent. The rest is a mix of conjunctions, prepositions, and so on.

1. The author of the article writes, "It is impossible to know for certain which language uses the largest number of words ..." Why is this true?

_____

_____

2. Which language is widely thought to be the language with the most words?

_____

3. English contains a very high percentage of borrowed words. List at least three languages from which you think English has adopted many words. Why did you choose these languages?

_____

_____

_____

4. People who write dictionaries are called *lexicographers*. Lexicographers are always working to update dictionaries. Explain why they must keep making revisions.

_____

_____

_____

_____

_____

_____

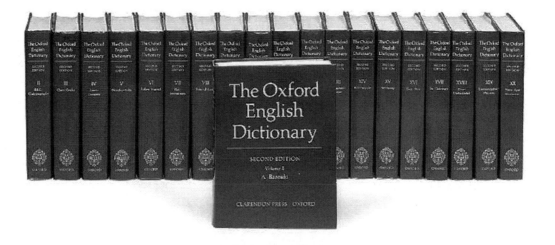

Name _____ Class _____ Date _____

Directions: The high number of words in English means that there are many words with roughly the same meaning. These words are called synonyms. The opposite of a synonym is an antonym. While a synonym means the same as a given word, an antonym means the opposite. For example, think about the word *peaceful*. Synonyms for peaceful include *serene* and *tranquil*. Antonyms for peaceful include *violent* and *disturbed*. Use this information to complete the following chart.

Synonym	Word	Antonym
	hot	
	dark	
	round	
	low	
	stop	
	happy	
	plump	
	whisper	
	wet	
	live	
	pull	

After completing the chart, check your answers with a thesaurus.

Name _____ Class _____ Date _____

When lexicographers write dictionaries, they don't make up words or definitions. A lexicographer's job is not to create language, but to record it. He or she must do research to find out which words people are using and what meanings these words have. Furthermore, lexicographers must find clear and concise ways to communicate all of this information. A dictionary wouldn't be very helpful if people couldn't understand what it was saying.

There are several pieces of standard information which dictionaries try to provide for every word. The first is usually the word's *pronunciation,* which will look like several letters and symbols grouped together near the beginning of the entry. The pronunciation section is intended to help you sound out a word, though you may need to refer to your dictionary's pronunciation key near the very front or back of your dictionary in order to understand all the symbols.

Next comes one of the most important pieces of information about a word—its part of speech. A *part of speech* simply means a category (such as noun, verb, adjective, adverb, or preposition) which indicates how a word should be used in a sentence. If you are not already familiar with these categories, your teacher can help you identify them during the exercise.

Next you will find a brief description of a word's history. This is called its *etymology.* You probably encountered information about the etymology of different words if you did the research project on borrowed words from Activity Sheet 2B.

Finally, each word must have at least one *definition.* If a word has multiple meanings, then the explanation of each main meaning will be given a number.

Directions: Use this activity to think about the information lexicographers gather. Pick five words that you use in your daily life or which refer to special actions or objects in a book that you've read. These should be words that have a particular meaning to you. Place them in the empty boxes in the column entitled "Word," and fill out the rest of the chart, using the example as a guide. Although lexicographers use special symbols for pronunciation, here you can just use the regular alphabet to spell out how the word should sound. Don't worry about figuring out your words' etymology. When you are done, look up two of your words (or your neighbor's words if yours aren't in the dictionary). Try to match the types of information you gave in the chart with the information you find in the dictionary. Use the dictionary's section on etymology to learn the histories of these two words.

Word	Pronunciation	Part of Speech	Definition
Read	"reed"	verb	to interpret or understand writing

NCTE/IRA
• 8, 9, 12

Time Required
• About two class periods

Teaching Tips

Students may work on the activity sheets individually, with a partner, or in small groups.

Activity Sheet 4A
• Emphasize the role of colonialism in the creation of Sranan Tongo.
• Use a map to help students locate Suriname.

Activity Sheet 4B
• Stress the importance of children in making a pidgin into a creole.
• Help students use Internet and library resources to locate foreign words.

Activity Sheet 4C
• Explain how English has been influenced by many other languages.
• Make sure your students understand the definitions of nouns, verbs, and homonyms. Help students notice particular homonyms' multiple meanings.

Answers

• *Activity Sheet 4A* 1. Sranan Tongo or Taki Taki; 2. over 400,000; 3. Sranan was originally created as a way for slaves, Dutch slave owners, and other inhabitants of Suriname to communicate with one another; 4. a language created by fusing together a mixture of other, already established languages.

• *Activity Sheet 4B* Answers will vary depending on the creoles chosen.

• *Activity Sheet 4C* Nouns: street, friction, platypus, fortress, child, driveway, car, dictionary; Verbs: anticipate, define, descend, discover, adore, prepare, understand, seek; Homonyms: race, jump, mold, count, bowl, bat, bear, flower, banter, boot, dock, kick, spill, trust, park.

Extension and Enrichment

• For an added challenge, have students research the origins of current English words and trace them back to their original languages and spellings.
• Students may also research Creole languages that are in the process of forming, such as Spanglish.

Visit <u>WorldRecordsBooks.com</u> for more images and activities!

Name _____ Class _____ Date _____

Directions: Read the article and complete the activities.

> The current language with the fewest words is Sranan Tongo, also known as Taki Taki. The *lexicon* of this language (that is, the list of its vocabulary) has only 340 words.
>
> Sranan is spoken in the country of Suriname, a colony planted by the Netherlands on the northeast side of South America. Because individuals of many different cultures and races live in Suriname, people who do not share the same primary language often have to find ways to communicate with one another. This need led to the invention of Sranan. Sranan is a creole and hence lends itself to being used as a common tongue between people of different ethnic groups. *Creoles* are languages created from a fusion of various other languages. Sranan, originally developed as a way for colonists, plantations owners, and slaves to communicate with each other, comes from a mix of English, Dutch, Portuguese, and various Central and West African Languages. This is why the lexicon of Sranan is so small. The original speakers would have needed the language to be as simple and easy to understand as possible. Eventually, children began to learn Sranan as their first speech, and this pieced-together tongue became a native language for the region. Today, more than 400,000 people speak Sranan, both in Suriname and in the Netherlands.

Suriname

1. What is the language with the fewest words?

   _____

2. How many people speak Sranan?

   _____

3. For what purpose was Sranan originally created?

   _____

   _____

4. What is a creole?

   _____

   _____

© 2013 Sunflower Education

Name _____ Class _____ Date _____

Perhaps one of the most interesting types of language to study from a linguistic point of view is a creole. A *creole* is a language that originates when groups speaking different languages need to communicate with one another and create a new, hybrid speech using pieces of their native tongues in order to do so. The speech formed by this first step is called a pidgin language. A *pidgin* language is usually a very simple mix that is spoken by adults as a second language. The next step is *nativization,* the process that occurs when children begin to learn the pidgin as their first language. By this point, the pidgin usually has a fully developed grammatical system and a large lexicon. It is at this stage, when children speak the language as natives, that it becomes a creole.

Directions: Because creoles are influenced so much by the languages from which they were created, it is often easy to see similarities between vocabulary in the offspring tongue and vocabulary in the parent tongues. For this activity, choose a creole and research its parent languages. For every English word in the left-hand column of the chart on the following page, try to find a word with the same meaning in the creole you picked. Next, try to find words with this same meaning in three of the creole's parent languages. (If there are only two parent languages, leave the last column blank.) Fill in the chart on the following page with these words, being careful to take note of any similarities among them.

cre·ole *noun* *krē-ōl*\\

a language that originates when groups speaking

different languages need to communicate with one

another and create a new, hybrid speech using pieces

of their native tongues in order to do so

Word in English	Word in Creole	Word in Parent Language #1	Word in Parent Language #2	Word in Parent Language #3
Example: Moon	Haitian Creole: Lalin	French: La lune	Spanish: La luna	Arabic: Amar
cat				
mother				
house				
dance				
tree				
brother				

Name _____ Class _____ Date _____

Words That Multitask

One of the reasons that creole languages like Sranan can function using only a few words is that one word may have many different meanings. Such a word may be pronounced the same way no matter which sense is intended, or its usage may involve different inflections or pronunciations for each of its different meanings. For example, the Sranan word "ti" may mean "hurt," "pain," "hot," or "hat," depending on how the speaker wishes to use it. When words are spelled the same way but contain multiple meanings, they are called *homonyms*. Homonyms are not just found in creoles and pidgins—they are also extremely common in English. This is because English, like these hybrid languages, constantly borrows words from other tongues. As a language evolves and changes over time, words that originally only sounded similar begin to be pronounced as if they were the same word. Eventually, many even come to be spelled identically.

Directions: Some of the most common homonyms in English function both as nouns and as verbs. Using the Venn Diagram, divide the following list of words into nouns, verbs, and homonyms that function as both. Remember, a *noun* is a person, place, or thing; a *verb* is an action word. Take your time and think carefully; words you are accustomed to think of as nouns may sometimes be used as verbs and vice versa.

> street, race, jump, anticipate, friction, mold, count, bowl, bat, define, descend, bear, flower, platypus, discover, fortress, adore, child, banter, boot, dock, driveway, kick, prepare, spill, understand, car, trust, park, seek, dictionary

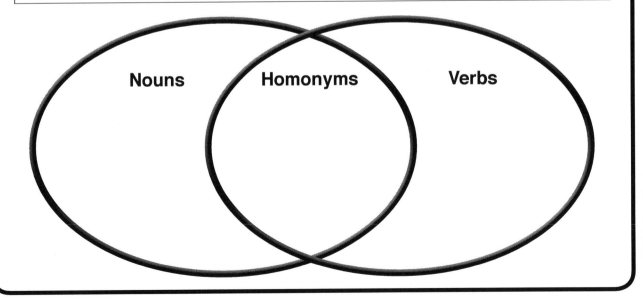

NCTE/IRA Standards
• 9, 12

Time Required
• About two class periods

Teaching Tips

Students may work on the activity sheets individually, with a partner, or with a small group.

Activity Sheet 5A
• Emphasize that writing was an important advance for state-level societies that participated in trade.
• Emphasize the transition from complex symbols to simple symbols.

Activity Sheet 5B
• Encourage students to deduce the meaning of each character from its shape.
• Emphasize the evolution of cuneiform from drawings to representative characters.

Activity Sheet 5C
• Remind students of the difference between symbols and alphabetic letters.
• Emphasize the utility of symbols.

Answers

• *Activity Sheet 5A* 1. phonetic and logographic; 2. Reward creative, thoughtful answers; 3. Written records helped traders keep track of their merchandise and profits; 4. Writing allowed a ruler to spread propaganda and keep records of different kinds. It would probably increase the knowledge of a ruler's advisers. Because writing can preserve one's thoughts and deeds long after death, a ruler might hope to gain lasting fame by commissioning autobiographical writings. In general, writing promoted communication and knowledge; 5. more than 1,000; It decreased because words became more simplified and streamlined.
• *Activity Sheet 5B* hand, bread, to walk, trees. Reward creative symbols.
• *Activity Sheet 5C* Answers will vary. Reward thoughtful responses.

Extension and Enrichment

• Students can conduct research to learn about other cuneiform characters.
• Students can make their own cuneiform-style writing using clay tablets and styli.

Visit WorldRecordsBooks.com for more images and activities!

Name _____ Class _____ Date _____

Directions: Read the article and answer the questions.

One of the most important and useful human inventions is writing. The written word is used for all kinds of communication, and it is one of the cornerstones of modern society.

Essentially, there are two kinds of writing systems: *phonetic* and *logographic*. Phonetic alphabets represent the sounds of a language; their building-blocks are letters which stand for consonant and vowel sounds, or sometimes combinations of the two. Logographic writing, on the other hand, represents units of meaning rather than of sound; in it, pictures and symbols stand for nouns and verbs.

The world's first writing system was *cuneiform*. Cuneiform developed around 3500 BCE in ancient Sumer, a civilization located in what is now southern Iraq. The word cuneiform means "wedge-shaped," and this name was chosen because cuneiform symbols were made by pressing a wedge-shaped reed into wet clay tablets. The first use of cuneiform appears to have been as a tool for traders to keep track of livestock and goods. Five symbols for "cow" meant five herds of cattle; three symbols for "sheep" represented three flocks of sheep. Thus, the world's earliest form of writing was also one of the world's earliest accounting systems.

As a new invention, cuneiform contained more than 1,000 different symbols, but as time went by it became much simpler. Within a few thousand years, the number of symbols had been reduced to about 400. The symbols themselves became less complicated, and the writing system became more uniform. These changes made cuneiform easier to learn and to use, and the subject matter it was used to express expanded to include more than matters of accounting and trade. The rulers of Sumer had their histories and achievements recorded, as well as information about their religion. By the time the phonetic alphabet was developed in Phoenicia, cuneiform was an extremely versatile and complex written language that had spread to nearly all of Sumer's neighbors.

Cuneiform

1. What are the two basic types of writing systems?

_____

2. What might be some of the advantages of a phonetic writing system over a logographic writing system?

_____

_____

_____

_____

3. Why was it important for ancient traders to be able to have a written record of their business?

_____

_____

_____

4. Why might writing be an important tool for a ruler?

_____

_____

_____

5. How many symbols did cuneiform have in the beginning? Why did the number of symbols decrease over time?

_____

_____

_____

Name _____ Class _____ Date _____

Over time, cuneiform characters developed from simple pictures into wedged-shaped symbols. For example, this is how the symbol for head evolved.

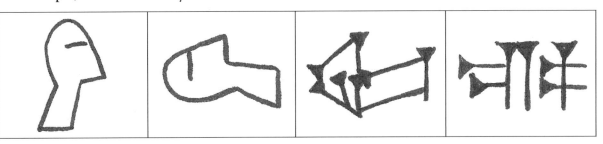

Directions: The examples below represent early cuneiform. See if you can match each symbol to its meaning.

Symbol	Meaning
	trees
	to walk
	hand
	bread

Directions: Now it's your turn to be creative. Invent and draw your own symbol for each word.

Symbol	Meaning
	god
	heaven
	man
	mountain
	drink
	plow
	sun
	woman

Symbols in Your Community

Activity Sheet 5C

Name _____ Class _____ Date _____

Even though English is notated using a phonetic alphabet, communication through logographic symbols is still common. Symbols can communicate simple but crucial knowledge quickly and therefore have not been entirely replaced; just think of all the street signs that use simple pictures to instantly convey their meanings. Generally, the symbols still in existence were initially chosen because they are easily identifiable and clearly correspond to that which they are intended to represent.

Directions: What are some things you read every day that are logographic rather than phonetic? As you walk around your school or community, take note of the symbols that you see and then record them in this table.

Symbol found	What does it mean?	Why do you think this symbol is used?

Symbol found	What does it mean?	Why do you think this symbol is used?

6. The World's First Computer Language

Plankalkül

NCTE/IRA Standards
- 4, 5, 9, 12

Time Requires
- About one class period

Teaching Tips
- Students may work on the activity sheets individually, with a partner, or with a small group.

Activity Sheet 6A
- Emphasize that unlike computers, people can often understand from context what a statement means even if it is ambiguous.
- Remind students about the universality of math.

Activity Sheet 6B
- Encourage students to be creative about coming up with ambiguous statements.

Activity Sheet 6C
- Encourage students to consider the advantages of different word orders.
- Connect this lesson to a review of the parts of speech.

Answers
- *Activity Sheet 6A* 1. Plankalkül; Konrad Zuse; 2. Computers require specific instructions that can't be confused; 3. Math is universal and unambiguous; 4. Answers will vary and may include the following response: Computer languages require an added degree of complexity to work on multiple types of computers.
- *Activity Sheet 6B* 1. It is unclear what the restaurant is serving and to whom; 2. Did they drive into a telephone pole accidentally, because they focused on a fly in the car, or were they trying to smash a fly on the telephone pole with their car?; 3. the month or a parade?; 4. He gave food to her dog, or he gave dog food to her?; 5. Figurative or literal?; 6. Who was in the green dress?; 7-12. Answers will vary. Encourage students to be creative.
- *Activity Sheet 6C* Reward clear and thoughtful responses.

Extension and Enrichment
- Students can learn basic computer programming.
- Discuss languages that are not dependent on word order, such as languages that rely more heavily on conjugations and declensions.

Visit WorldRecordsBooks.com for more images and activities!

Name _____ Class _____ Date _____

Directions: Read the article and complete the activities.

The world's first computer language was called Plankalkül, which means "plan calculus" in German. Plankalkül was created between 1943 and 1945 by Konrad Zuse. At the time, it was intended to run engineering programs, but it wasn't actually put to use until 1998.

Computers need their own languages. Unlike people, computers need to be told exactly what to do; computers require a precise language without ambiguity. *Ambiguity* is when words or phrases can have more than one meaning. For example, in English the word "watch" can be either a synonym for "look" or it can refer to a time-telling accessory. Computers need specific instructions, so programmers write computer languages without ambiguity.

Because computers need specific instructions, their languages are often based on or very strongly influenced by math or logic. "2+2=4" only means one thing. Computer languages are built on mathematics more advanced than arithmetic, however. For example, Konrad Zuse used algebra to create Plankalkül.

1. What was the first computer language? Who created it?

_____

2. Why can't computer languages be ambiguous?

_____

_____

3. Why are a lot of computer languages based on math?

_____

4. Early computer languages only worked on a specific type of computer. Why do you think this is so?

_____

_____

Konrad Zuse

Name _____ Class _____ Date _____

Ambiguity is one of the most interesting facets of language. It can be misleading, but also lead to some funny statements. For example, the comedic actor Groucho Marx is famously quoted as saying, "I once shot an elephant in my pajamas. How he got in my pajamas I'll never know." This quote is considered funny precisely because its initial ambiguity is misleading. The first sentence of the statement sets up expectations that Groucho was in his pajamas when he shot an elephant. In the second sentence, however, Groucho reveals that it was the elephant, and not himself, that was wearing his pajamas. Our surprise, coupled with the ridiculousness of the alternative interpretation, creates the statement's humor.

Directions: Explain how the following sentences demonstrate ambiguity in English, and then create and explain some ambiguous statements of your own.

---

1. We don't just serve hamburgers. We serve people.

Explain:

---

2. Attempting to kill a fly, we drove into a telephone pole.

Explain:

---

3. March Planned for Next August

Explain:

---

4. He gave her dog food.

Explain:

---

5. They let the cat out of the bag.

Explain:

---

6. The professor called his cousin in a green dress.

Explain:

7.

Explain:

8.

Explain:

9.

Explain:

10.

Explain:

11.

Explain:

12.

Explain:

Name _____ Class _____ Date _____

What makes up a language? Two major components of language are semantics and syntax. *Semantics* deals with the meaning of all the words in a language. *Syntax*, also called *grammar*, is the way words can be put together. So when Konrad Zuse developed Plankalkül, the world's first computer language, he didn't just think about what the words meant. He also had to develop rules for how the words could be put together.

In English the words, "blanket couch a found the I under," make no sense. When they're rearranged, you know what they mean. "I found a blanket under the couch." If we need rules for how words can be put together, it makes sense that computers might rely on rules for *word order* even more. Word order is not the only part of grammar, but it is an important part.

Directions: Konrad Zuse designed Plankalkül for engineering programming. If he had used English words, how might he have changed the word order of a sentence to fit engineering purposes? Action sentences in English normally follow this order: subject, verb, direct object. Other languages use different orders like subject, direct object, verb. Maybe for engineering programs it would make the most sense to have the direct object come first. Engineers need to know what materials they are using. Think of something you are interested in, and how you could reorder sentences for that activity. Write a paragraph in the new word order you come up with about the topic you selected.

_____

_____

_____

_____

_____

_____

_____

_____

_____

_____

NCTE/IRA Standards
• 4, 5, 7, 8, 9, 12

Time Required
• About one class period

Teaching Tips

Students may work on the activity sheets individually, with a partner, or in small groups.

Activity Sheet 7A
• Emphasize the amount of linguistic diversity in the world and that the official language of a country does not necessarily represent all the languages spoken within that country.
• Be sure to explain the terms "bilingual" and "multilingual."

Activity Sheet 7B
• Emphasize the role of colonialism in making English, Spanish, and French the world's major linguas francas.
• Stress the fact that English is currently the lingua franca for the fields of business, science, and technology.

Activity Sheet 7C
• Emphasize that most students' ancestors did not speak English upon arriving in this country.
• Encourage students to think for themselves and gather as much information as possible before making their decisions.

Answers

• *Activity Sheet 7A* 1. There are between 4,000 and 10,000 languages in the world. We can never know an exact number because languages are constantly changing, being created, and going extinct; 2. The Republic of India is made up of many different ethnic and religious groups who all speak different languages; 3. A registered population of speakers means that researchers have found actual people who speak the language on a daily basis. This is important because if no one uses a language to communicate anymore, it is no longer a living language.
• *Activity Sheet 7B* 1-2. Reward thoughtful, well-written answers.
• *Activity Sheet 7C* Answers will vary based on the community and the individual students.

Extension and Enrichment

• To add more depth to this lesson, have the students research the history of India or Papua New Guinea, paying special attention to the diversity of the population.
• For a more local approach, have your students go out into their communities to log how many different languages they hear spoken.

Visit WorldRecordsBooks.com for more images and activities!

Name _____ Class _____ Date _____

Directions: Read the article and complete the activities.

How many languages do you usually hear as you go about your day? Depending on where you live in the United States, the number may range from 1 to 50! However, even people who come into contact with fifty different languages a day are still only scratching the surface of the world's languages. Though we can never be certain because the number changes constantly, most experts agree that there are between 4,000 and 10,000 languages in the world today. A recent list of the world's languages noted that there are about 6,000 languages with a registered population of speakers. Many of these languages can overlap and exist within the same country.

Papua New Guinea, a small island country in Southeast Asia, is home to more than 820 different languages and multiple dialects of those languages, making it the country containing the most languages in the world. In fact, 11.86% of all the world's languages are spoken within its borders. On average, each language has about 7,000 speakers. Despite its linguistic diversity, Papua New Guinea possesses only three *official* languages: English, Tok Pisin, and Motu. An official language is given special legal stature by the government.

The country with the most official languages is the Republic of India, which uses an astounding 24 different languages in official capacities: Assamese, Bengali, Bodo, Dogri, English, Gujarati, Hindi, Kannada, Kashmiri, Konkani, Maithili, Malayalam, Marathi, Meitei, Nepali, Oriya, Eastern Panjabi, Sanskrit, Santali, Sindhi, Tamil, Telugu, and Urdu. There only appear to be 23 here. Though Hindi and English are generally the languages most uniformly used across India, the remaining 22 are used regionally and in their home states. There are so many languages to be recognized because the Republic of India is a large, diverse country, stretching over a million square miles. The country is composed of many ethnicities and religions, and the diversity of the recognized languages reflects this.

Languages of India

Language	Number of Speakers
Bhojpuri	33,099,497
Rajasthani	18,355,613
Magadh/Magah	13,978,565
Chhattisgarh	13,260,186
Haryanvi	7,997,192
Marwari	7,936,183
Malvi	5,565,167
Mewari	5,091,697
Khorth/Khotta	4,725,927
Bundeli/Bundelkhan	3,072,147
Bagheli/Baghel Khan	2,865,011
Pahari	2,832,825
Laman/Lambadi	2,707,562
Awadhi	2,529,308
Harauti	2,462,867
Garhwali	2,267,314
Nimadi	2,148,146
Sadan/Sadri	2,044,776
Kumauni	2,003,783
Dhundhari	1,871,130
Surgujia	1,458,533
Bagri Rajasthani	1,434,123
Banjari	1,259,821
Nagpuria (Varhadi)	1,242,586
Surjapuri	1,217,019
Kangri	1,122,843

1. Approximately how many languages are there in the world today? Why can we never know an exact number?

_____

_____

_____

_____

2. Why are there so many different languages recognized in the Republic of India?

_____

_____

_____

_____

3. The article states that there are about 6,000 languages with a registered population of speakers. What does this mean, and why would it be important?

_____

_____

_____

_____

_____

_____

_____

_____

Language Bridges

Activity Sheet 7B

Name _____ Class _____ Date _____

If you look at a list of the official languages of all the countries in the world, you will find that English is a common occurrence on the list. That is because, due to the lasting effects of British colonialism, English acts as a "lingua franca" in many parts of the world.

A *lingua franca* is a language that acts as a bridging language between groups that have different mother tongues. For example, in the state of Chiapas, Mexico, there are many different groups of Mayans who speak different native languages. When a person who speaks Tzotzil meets with a person whose native tongue is Ch'ol, they will often use Spanish as a bridge language to communicate with one another.

In most of the developed world, linguas francas tend overwhelmingly to be old colonial languages: English, Spanish, French, German, and Portuguese. The reasons for this are complicated, but the main one is that colonialism drew together various tribes and groups of people who often spoke radically different languages and ordinarily would not have formed a single country. When colonies became independent countries, choosing the colonial language as the lingua franca rather than one of many indigenous languages was often viewed as a way to avoid the political difficulties of promoting one indigenous language above another.

Directions: Answer the following questions.

1. Though English is the *de facto* language of the United States, meaning that it exists "in fact" or without legal authority, the U.S. has no law stating that English is the official language. Does this mean that English is a lingua franca in the U.S.? Why or why not?

   _____

   _____

   _____

   _____

2. What are your experiences with linguas francas? Have you ever used a bridge language in order to communicate with someone who speaks a different native tongue than you do?

   _____

   _____

   _____

   _____

Name _____ Class _____ Date _____

With the exception of Native Americans, the population of the United States of America is made entirely of people whose ancestors came from somewhere else within relatively recent history. Usually, when those ancestors immigrated to the United States, they spoke their native language and only a little or no English. Partially in homage to this, the United States has no official national language. Though English is the *de facto* language and is the most widely spoken language in the country, nearly 20% of Americans speak a language other than English at home. That's almost one in five Americans!

This has become a contentious topic, and many people believe that English should be made the official national language of the United States. In many cases, this would mean that all official documents and governmental business would have to be in English, and translation into other languages would no longer be provided.

Directions: Should English be established as the official language of the United States? Why?

_____

_____

_____

_____

_____

_____

_____

_____

_____

_____

_____

_____

_____

8. The World's Most Endangered Language

Yuchi

NCTE/IRA Standards
• 9, 12

Time Required
• About one class period

Teaching Tips

Students may work on the activity sheets individually, with a partner, or in small groups.

Activity Sheet 8A
• Emphasize languages' cultural importance.
• Explain that many languages are dying out because people are switching to other languages, such as English or Mandarin.

Activity Sheet 8B
• Emphasize that English is not the official language of the U.S. but rather the *de facto* language and that, therefore, any language could be used in schools and government.
• Demonstrate where Hawaii is on a map.
• Explain what an immersion school is.

Activity Sheet 8C
• Combine this activity with a brief history lesson of the area so that students know which Native American groups lived there.
• Utilize as many outside sources as possible—maps, the local Historical Society, guest speakers, etc.

Answers

• *Activity Sheet 8A* 1. Because language holds all of the most important aspects of a culture: traditions, beliefs, religion, stories, and history; 2. Language diversity is important because it is a human heritage, and it helps to preserve and maintain the identity of cultural groups; 3. 80% of the world's languages face extinction in the next 100 years; 4. A moribund language is a language that children no longer learn; 5. Five elderly people currently speak Yuchi.
• *Activity Sheet 8B* Reward thoughtful answers.
• *Activity Sheet 8C* Answers will vary depending on the location.

Extension and Enrichment

• Students can conduct independent research and provide presentations on an endangered or extinct language of their choice.
• Guest speakers, experts, or speakers of an endangered language can be brought in to give presentations.

Visit WorldRecordsBooks.com for more images and activities!

Name _____ Class _____ Date _____

Directions: Read the article and answer the questions.

Look around you. Everything you see and feel is processed through language. Language gives shape and recognition to your experiences and gives you memory. It provides a framework for the thoughts and beliefs that make you who you are. Just as language shapes and molds individuals, it also provides the framework for cultures. Language is the medium through which a culture's stories, religion, history, and beliefs are passed down from generation to generation. In a sense, language can hold a culture's soul. It is for this reason that the United Nations Educational, Scientific and Cultural Organization (UNESCO) has designated language an "intangible heritage" whose diversity must be protected.

As many as 80% of the world's languages are in danger of going extinct within the next 50-100 years. Linguists have determined that there are three categories of pre-extinct language. The first includes safe languages. Safe languages are languages that children will likely still be learning a century from now. The second category is endangered languages. Endangered languages are languages that children will probably not be speaking in a century. Researchers estimate that 60-80% of the world's languages are endangered languages. The final and most urgent category is moribund languages. Moribund languages are languages that children don't speak today—languages that aren't being taught to new generations. Approximately 15-30% of the world's languages are moribund languages. They will die out and become extinct as the current speakers grow old and die.

When it comes to determining which languages are most in danger of extinction, the number of speakers is less important than the age distribution of the speakers. For a language to survive, it is critical that new generations learn it. The most recent list of nearly-extinct languages states that there are five-hundred and twelve on the verge of dying out. All are languages spoken by very few people, all of whom are elderly. Though it is difficult to choose one over the rest as most in danger, Yuchi, a Native American language, is certainly on the verge of disappearance. Yuchi is currently spoken only by five elderly people in Oklahoma, USA and is an isolate, which means that it is related to no other language on Earth. Efforts are currently being made to teach the language to children and record words and syntax, but will there be enough time to save the Yuchi language before it is too late?

1. Why has UNESCO designated language as a human heritage?

_____

_____

_____

_____

_____

2. Why is language diversity important?

_____

_____

_____

_____

_____

3. What percentage of the world's languages face extinction within the next 100 years?

_____

4. What is a moribund language?

_____

_____

_____

5. How many people currently speak Yuchi?

_____

_____

Back From the Brink: Reviving Languages

Activity Sheet 8B

Name _____ Class _____ Date _____

On the island of Niihau in Hawaii, children awaken early and prepare for school, just like children all over Hawaii and the rest of the United States do. However, for the many children on Niihau who attend immersion schools, the lessons aren't in English; they are in the island's native language, also called Niihau. These immersion schools have been growing in popularity and are part of the movement to revitalize native Hawaiian languages and, through them, Hawaiian culture. Revitalization occurs when groups make an effort to save an endangered language from extinction. It usually entails extensively documenting the language from the few remaining original speakers and then ensuring that the language is passed on to the next generation, usually through implementing the language in schools, official domains, and everyday life. Efforts such as this are taking place all over the world today as concerned communities race to save their distinct languages from extinction.

Thinking Critically

1. Do you think that language revitalization is important? Why or why not?

_____

_____

_____

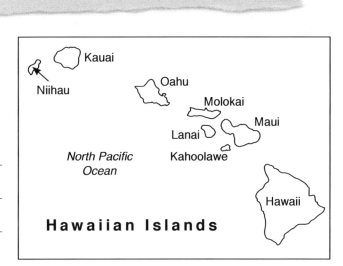

2. Would you like to attend an immersion school? Why or why not? What are some possible pros and cons of attending a language immersion school?

_____

_____

_____

_____

_____

© 2013 Sunflower Education

Name _____ Class _____ Date _____

Though today most Native Americans live on reservations, before colonialism nearly every part of the United States was inhabited by a nation, and generally each nation had its own language or dialect. It is estimated that before Columbus arrived there were as many as 280 distinct languages in North America. Today, more than 191 of those original languages are either endangered or extinct.

Directions: As a part of their efforts to preserve endangered languages, UNESCO has many resources that people can use to learn about endangered languages in their area. Using www.unesco.org/culture/languages-atlas, determine whether there are any endangered or extinct languages in your region. Use this research to fill out the chart below.

Endangered and Extinct Languages in _____				
(Name of Your Region)				
Name of Language	Number of Current Speakers	Spoken By: (Tribe or Group)	Extinct or Endangered	Language Family

9. The World's Oldest Living Language
Aboriginal or Khoisan

NCTE/IRA Standards
• 4, 5, 9, 12

Time Required
• About two class periods

Teaching Tips

Students may work on the activity sheets individually, with a partner, or in small groups.

Activity Sheet 9A
• Explain the term "Aborigine."
• Emphasize why designating one living language as the oldest is controversial.

Activity Sheet 9B
• Ensure student understanding of *slang*.
• Explain that slang used in a particular profession is called *jargon*.

Activity Sheet 9C
• Emphasize that oral tradition is still extremely important in many cultures today.
• Explain to students that much of their culture and family history is passed down through oral tradition.
• Encourage students to further research their own oral histories.

Answers

• *Activity Sheet 9A* 1. Because there is no tangible evidence that can be dated or studied by archaeologists; 2. Latin isn't technically considered a "living" language; 3. No new languages came into contact with Australian languages for 60,000 years. Australian languages remained relatively "pure" and without outside influence; 4. They were fairly isolated and come from the region that has been inhabited by humans the longest; 5. Spoken language had to have been around for a long time before the written language was developed, and many spoken languages have no writing.
• *Activity Sheet 9B* Answers will vary. Reward thoughtful responses.
• *Activity Sheet 9C* Answers will vary but should demonstrate effort and understanding.

Extension and Enrichment

• Students can participate in their own debate about which language should be designated as the oldest one living.
• Students can prepare their own visual representations of language change and movement on a different continent.

Visit <u>WorldRecordsBooks.com</u> for more images and activities!

Name _____ Class _____ Date _____

Directions: Read the article and complete the activities.

The age of a spoken language is extremely difficult to determine. Once words are said aloud, they leave no physical trace, no tangible evidence for archaeologists to find and study later. However, by studying how different languages and dialects relate to one another, linguists can often assign approximate ages to languages and determine when they emerged, even if the language is no longer spoken or has changed significantly. Still, because languages leave no artifacts unless written down, it is hard to provide physical proof of such ages. For this reason, it is very controversial to give one language the title of "World's Oldest Living Language." There are many languages that could possibly earn this distinction, including Latin, Greek, Hebrew, Mayan, Chinese, Tamil, Sanskrit, the languages of the Australian Aborigines, and the South African bushman languages of the Khoisan family. All except the Aborigine and Khoisan languages have writings and written literature that date back to at least two thousand years ago, and all are still used in some form today. So how do we narrow down the list?

Latin is technically no longer a "living" language. Though it is used in religious ceremonies, children no longer learn it as a primary language from their parents. Though Chinese, Hebrew, and Greek are indeed ancient languages, the versions of each that are still spoken today are radically different from the classical versions. Chinese in particular has gone through several reconstructions due to the original language being lost or disconnected at times. Tamil and Sanskrit are particularly problematic because each evolved at around the same time and from different language families. Written literature from each has been dated to at least three thousand years ago, which means that the spoken languages are even older. Mayan is still spoken today by approximately seven million people in Central America and the language is at least five thousand years old—probably much older. However, researchers know very little about Mayan culture in that era, so there is almost no concrete evidence.

A San Bushman

Though the Aborigines of Australia and the tribes of Southern Africa have no written records of their languages, geography and natural history indicate that the oldest living languages are likely to be found among these peoples. For more than sixty-thousand years, a group of people called Aborigines has inhabited Australia and had little to no contact with the outside world until quite recently. This means that the Aboriginal languages are ancient and haven't been influenced by other languages or language families. Though it is difficult to tell without written records, other archaeological evidence such as art and storytelling makes it clear that Aboriginal culture has maintained a level of continuity for tens of thousands of years. This makes it extremely likely that their language has changed relatively little compared to other languages during that time.

Africa, often referred to as "the birthplace of humanity," is where human beings first evolved. All of the world's languages can be eventually traced back to a mother tongue in Africa. Some researchers believe that a direct descendent of this ancient mother tongue can be found in the Khoisan language family. This language family, also called the "click languages," is known for its use of a clicking noise in place of certain vowels. Theoretically, one of these Khoisan languages could be hundreds of thousands of years old.

1. Why is the age of a spoken language difficult to determine?

_____

2. Why isn't Latin considered the oldest living language?

_____

_____

3. How did Australia's historic isolation contribute to the continuity of its languages?

_____

_____

4. Why is it likely that the Khoisan languages are the oldest in the world?

_____

_____

5. Why can't, as the only tangible evidence available, written languages be solely used to determine the age of a spoken language?

_____

_____

Slang

Activity Sheet 9B

Name _____ Class _____ Date _____

All languages change over time. Some change dramatically, and quickly. Others change little, over long periods of time. But they all change.

Why do languages change? Social and economic changes, such as colonization and migration, can cause change. New technologies and industries require new words. Perhaps the chief driver of change is the way individuals speak. People's age, where they live, their social status and other factors affect how they use their language. Over time, interaction among people spread slightly different uses of language, and a change takes place.

One source of change is slang. Slang is a type of language that uses informal words and phrases in new ways. All languages have slang, which is more often spoken than written. Slang can be formed from new words, or by giving new meanings to words. Over time, some slang words and expressions become part of the formal language. Hoax is a word that started out as slang. So is the word strenuous, pushover, and skyscraper.

Directions: Complete the table.

Slang Word or Expression I Use	What it Means	Will it Become Part of Formal English? Why or Why Not?	Should it Become Part of Formal English? Why or Why Not?

© 2013 Sunflower Education

Activity Sheet 9C

Name _____ Class _____ Date _____

When you learn the history of your country, chances are you turn to a book or other written resource. When you want something to be remembered for a long time, you probably write it down. In contemporary Western culture, writing is how knowledge is passed from one person to another.

However, there are other, older ways of preserving knowledge that many cultures around the world still utilize. Oral traditions, testimony, or lore are how the ancients passed information from one generation to the next. Usually, the history, traditions, and beliefs of a culture would be contained within stories, songs, and myths and then painstakingly taught by elder to child, thus ensuring that knowledge would be preserved. People were trained from childhood to be able to remember huge amounts of information verbatim and to be able to repeat that information when necessary.

Many of Western civilization's most treasured works of literature were originally oral traditions that were only written down after hundreds of years of verbal transmission. For instance, most of the epics of various cultures, such as The Iliad, The Odyssey, Ramayana, and Beowolf were oral traditions for many years before being preserved in the written form that we recognize today.

A Hausa Griot performs in Niger. Griots are West African storytellers and musicians who maintain oral traditions.

Directions: Think of a story or bit of folklore that your family shares. It can be something that a relative tells you, a bedtime story, or a bit of family history. Divide up into small groups and take turns sharing your stories. Use this experience to help you complete the rest of this worksheet.

1. What kind of story did you share? Is it something that you've heard more than once from an elder? Did it have some kind of lesson or moral attached?

   _____

   _____

2. Do you think oral tradition accurately preserves stories, or would they change over time?

   _____

   _____

10. The World's Longest Word
Pneumonoultramicroscopicsilicovolcanokoniosis

NCTE/IRA Standards
• 9, 12

Time Required
• About one class period

Teaching Tips
Students may work on the activity sheets individually, with a partner, or in small groups.

Activity Sheet 10A
• Emphasize that few really long words occur in everyday use.
• Remind students that by understanding the pieces that make up a word, they can understand words they've never seen before.

Activity Sheet 10B
• Encourage students to concentrate on the words they have already seen with these prefixes and suffixes.
• Remind students to be as specific as possible.

Activity Sheet 10C
• Encourage students to be creative.

Answers
• **Activity Sheet 10A** 1. Pneumonoultramicroscopicsilicovolcanokoniosis, 45; 2. a few letters added to the beginning of a word that add meaning, answers will vary; 3. a few letters added to the end of a word that add meaning, answers will vary.
• **Activity Sheet 10B** prefix, not; prefix, self; suffix, the study of; suffix, past tense; prefix, bad; prefix, below; suffix, the belief in; suffix, without; prefix, after; prefix, three; suffix, the fear of.
• **Activity Sheet 10C** Reward clear, thoughtful responses.

Extension and Enrichment
• Students can study the roots of many long words. Particularly in English, a basic Latin vocabulary can be very helpful.
• Students can participate in spelling bees to further their vocabulary and provide motivation.

Visit <u>WorldRecordsBooks.com</u> for more images and activities!

Name _____ Class _____ Date _____

Directions: Read the article and complete the activities.

What is the longest word you've ever heard? When you were little did you ever hear "Supercalifragilisticexpialidocious"? Or maybe more recently you were introduced to "Antidisestablishmentarianisms." At 34 and 29 letters, these are both long words, but neither of them is the world's longest. The longest word to ever appear in an English dictionary is Pneumonoultramicroscopicsilicovolcano-koniosis. It's more commonly known as "grinder's disease," and refers to a lung condition caused by inhaling very small particles of silicon. This word was created specifically to be a long word, as there is a much shorter synonym, silicosis.

But even that 45-letter word is not the world's longest. The longest word to appear in literature is Lopadotemachoselachogaleokranioleipsanodrimhypotrimmatosilphioparao melitokatakechymenokichlepikossyphophattoperisteralektryonoptekephalliokigklopel eiolagoiosiraiobaphetraganopterygon. In the original Greek, this word has 171 letters! It's a made-up food from Aristophenes' play *Assemblywomen*. That's a mouthful.

How do you make a word that long? You use prefixes and suffixes. A prefix is a specific combination of letters added to the beginning of a word that add meaning. If you add "pre-" to the beginning of "history," you get a word that means before history. A suffix does the same thing by adding the letters to the end of the word. One of the most common suffixes in English is "-s." It changes for example, pizza to pizzas. Singulars into plurals.

The medical field uses many prefixes. Some people would argue that the world's longest word should be the scientific name of a protein. Theoretically, protein names can go on infinitely by continuing to add more prefixes and suffixes.

1. How many letters are in the longest English word?

_____

2. What is a prefix? List three common prefixes.

_____

_____

3. What is a suffix? List three common suffixes.

_____

_____

Name _____ Class _____ Date _____

Prefixes and suffixes allow us to create new words using words that already exist. By combining words and pieces of words that we already know, we don't have to learn or create completely new ways of putting letters together. Prefixes and suffixes also help because there are only so many sounds the human mouth can make. If we never reused a combination, we would quickly run out of sounds.

Directions: Look at the list of prefixes and suffixes below. Think about the prefixes and suffixes you already know and how they change the words they are a part of. Then complete the table.

	Prefix or Suffix?	Meaning
a-, an-		
auto-		
-logy		
-ed		
mal-		
sub-		
-ism		
-less		
post-		
tri-		
-phobia		

After completing the table, check your answers in a dictionary.

Building A Word

Activity Sheet 10C

Name _____ Class _____ Date _____

Pneumonoultramicroscopicsilicovolcanokoniosis was coined in an attempt to be the longest word in the English language—and it worked! Even though there was already a perfectly good word meaning the exact same thing, pneumonoultramicroscopicsilicovolcanokoniosis made it.

Directions: If other people can coin a huge word, why can't you? Use the prefixes from Activity Sheet 10B along with all the others you can think of to create the longest word you can. You should understand it, and be able to explain what your word means.

Your Word:

_____

_____

_____

_____

_____

Definition of Your Word:

_____

_____

_____

_____

_____

_____

_____

_____

World Records of Literature

NCTE/IRA Standards
• 4, 5, 9, 11, 12

Time Required
• About two class periods

Teaching Tips
Students may work on the activity sheets individually, with a partner, or in small groups.

Activity Sheet 11A
• Emphasize that there have been stories for longer than we know.
• Remind students about the speed with which paper decays.

Activity Sheet 11B
• Encourage students to think about factors other than word order.

Activity Sheet 11C
• Encourage students to be creative.
• Look at how the same elements of a story can be put together in a wide variety of ways.

Answers
• **Activity Sheet 11A** 1. Scholars do not know the name of the book because it was written in Etruscan, an ancient language which people no longer know how to read; 2. Bulgaria; Etruscan; 3. Answers will vary. Reward thoughtful responses.

• **Activity Sheet 11B** vos—you; Amor—Cupid; approbanter—sneeze; Si—if; avais—had; voiture—car; chis-sol—toothbrush; pil-yo—need; sae—new; heroe—flamingo; kuogelea—swim; bwawa—pool.

• **Activity Sheet 11C** Answers will vary. Reward creative responses.

Extension and Enrichment
• Students can conduct research on other texts that might be classified as the world's oldest book.
• Students can learn about the Etruscan civilization and why Etruscans were some of the first people to create books.

Visit <u>WorldRecordsBooks.com</u> for more images and activities!

Name _____ Class _____ Date _____

Directions: Read the article and complete the activities.

No one knows what the first book was about or who wrote it. Perhaps it exists undiscovered or unrecognized to this day, though it was probably destroyed by decay or circumstance long ago. Out of the ancient stories and books that have survived and are known today, the oldest are the *Epic of Gilgamesh,* a tale which was being told about 4,000 years ago (though it wasn't made into a book until much, much later in history), and a six-page book discovered in Bulgaria and made of solid gold. At 2,500 years old, this is the oldest book we know about that still physically exists.

The name of the solid gold book remains a mystery. It was written in the language of the Etruscans, a people who lived in northern Italy before the time of the Roman Empire. Little is known about them, and theirs is one in a relatively small collection of languages which modern scholars are still unable to read.

One day this may change. Over time, remarkable progress has been made in the study of ancient writings, and it is possible that we will eventually understand Etruscan. One example of an ancient writing form which scholars can now translate is Egyptian hieroglyphs. It was unknown how to read them until the discovery of the Rosetta Stone, a slab of rock on which the same story was written in ancient Greek, Demotic Egyptian, and Egyptian hieroglyphs. Because scholars could read ancient Greek, they knew what the hieroglyphs were supposed to be saying and hence were able to figure out how hieroglyphs were used.

Gilgamesh, the fifth king of Uruk.

Although we can't currently read it, the oldest known book does give us a few clues about its subject matter. The text is illustrated with pictures of a mermaid, a harp, soldiers, and a horse and rider.

1. What is the title of the world's oldest known surviving book?

_____

2. Where was this book found? What language is it in?

_____

3. In modern times, we think of gold as something of extreme value. Why do you think people 2,500 years ago would make a book out of gold?

_____

Name _____ Class _____ Date _____

Directions: Scientists used the Rosetta Stone to decipher what Egyptian hieroglyphs mean. Use the sentences below to guess what the words in the chart mean.

"Sternuat Amor approbanter in vos."

May Cupid sneeze favorably on you.

—Latin

"Si j'avais une nouvelle voiture aussi!"

If only I had a new car too!

—French

"Naneun sae chis-sol i pil-yo"

I need a new toothbrush.

—Korean

"Heroe ilikuwa kuogelea katika bwawa binafsi."

The flamingo was swimming in the private pool.

—Swahili

Word	Meaning
vos	
Amor	
approbanter	
Si	
avais	
voiture	

chis-sol	
pil-yo	
sae	
heroe	
kuogelea	
bwawa	

The Rosetta Stone

Name _____ Class _____ Date _____

What can you learn about a story from the included illustrations? Scholars have had many opportunities to compare the subject matter of texts with that of the pictures which accompany them. In fact, most civilizations that use writing have used illustrations in at least some of their texts. In the Middle Ages, for example, European monks whose job it was to copy long books by hand would create intricate pictures and designs in the margins. The manuscripts they created are called "illuminated" texts. The pictures accompanying a text often align closely with the content of the written story.

Directions: Think about the illustrations found in the oldest known surviving book. As you may recall, these included a horse and rider, a mermaid, soldiers, and a harp. Write a creative short story that incorporates all of these elements.

_____

_____

_____

_____

_____

_____

_____

_____

_____

_____

_____

_____

_____

_____

NCTE/IRA Standards
• 4, 5, 11, 12

Time Required
• About one class period

Teaching Tips
Students may work on the activity sheets individually, with a partner, or with a small group.

Activity Sheet 12A
• Emphasize that plays are meant to be performed.
• Remind students of the longevity of stories.

Activity Sheet 12B
• Go over the elements of theater before having students complete the activity.

Activity Sheet 12C
• Use your judgment about how to structure this activity. Writing and performing even a very short play can be a difficult undertaking, and students may need a fair amount of assistance.
• Encourage students to be creative.
• Be aware of group dynamics as the students work together. Make sure the students who are not performing at any given time behave as a considerate, supportive audience.

Answers
• *Activity Sheet 12A* 1. *The Persians*; Aeschylus; 2. No, Aeschylus composed plays for 25 years before writing *The Persians*, and plays were performed for a long time before people even began to write them down; 3. The ancient Greeks and the Persians were military opponents.
• *Activity Sheet 12B* 1. C; 2. G; 3. I; 4. A; 5. B; 6. J; 7. E; 8. F; 9. D; 10. K; 11. H
• *Activity Sheet 12C* Reward creative writing, acting, and directing. Ensure that the environment in which the plays are performed is supportive.

Extension and Enrichment
• Students can engage in a class discussion about the strengths and weaknesses of live theater as a medium for expressing different thoughts and feelings.
• Students can go to a local play and write their own play reviews.
• Students can participate in a school play or put on a play if one is not readily available.

Visit <u>WorldRecordsBooks.com</u> for more images and activities!

Name _____ Class _____ Date _____

Directions: Read the article and complete the activities.

The oldest surviving play is entitled *The Persians* and was written by Aeschylus, a famous ancient Greek playwright. Though *The Persians* is the oldest play whose manuscript we have, we know that there were many plays that were even older. People acted out stories long before anyone wrote them down, and records show that Aeschylus himself had been composing plays for 25 years before completing *The Persians.*

It is fitting that a work by Aeschylus is the oldest play to survive. The ancient Greeks made significant contributions to the development of theater, many of which are still used in the writing and production of plays today. For example, the formal concepts of tragedy and comedy, the setup of many of our theaters, and even the word "theater" came from the ancient Greeks.

The Persians may have been one of the first plays to look at a war from an enemy's point of view. In it, Aeschylus portrays Persian characters reacting to their recent and momentous defeat in a battle with the Greeks; it is likely that Aeschylus valued the ability of people on one side of a conflict to understand the thoughts and feelings of people on the other side. Plays which venture into this kind of uncomfortable territory are not always popular since people may dislike being encouraged to consider an enemy's perspective. Theater has a long-standing history of trying to get people to look at the world in a different way.

Epidaurus, Greek theater

1. What is the world's oldest extant play? Who wrote it?

_____

2. Was the world's oldest extant play the world's first play? How do you know?

_____

3. The world's oldest extant play looked at the Persians' point of view. What kind of relationship did the ancient Greeks have with the Persians?

_____

Name _____ Class _____ Date _____

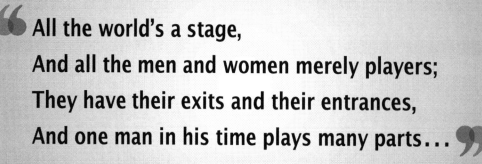

" All the world's a stage,
And all the men and women merely players;
They have their exits and their entrances,
And one man in his time plays many parts... "

You've probably heard this famous line from Shakespeare's *As You Like It*. You may have even said it before. But how far can you take this metaphor? Learn a little more about the theater before you decide.

Directions: Match the elements of theater on the left with their meaning on the right.

Theatrical Element	Meaning
_____ 1. cast	A. the words one character is supposed to say before the next character speaks
_____ 2. character	B. a play that ends happily
_____ 3. script	C. all of the actors and actresses in a play
_____ 4. line	D. speaking like people from a particular place
_____ 5. comedy	E. a person who plays a character in a play
_____ 6. tragedy	F. speaking every sound clearly

_____ 7. actor	G. a person from the world of the play
_____ 8. articulation	H. the frame around the stage
_____ 9. accent	I. the play in written form
_____ 10. upstage	J. a play with a sad ending
_____ 11. proscenium arch	K. the direction away from the audience

The masks of drama—comedy and tragedy.
The laughing face is Thalia, the ancient Greek muse
of comedy. The crying face is Melpomene,
the ancient Greek muse of tragedy.

Name _____ Class _____ Date _____

Plays are unlike most other types of literature in that, though they may be *read* like books, they are actually meant to be *performed*. Reading Hamlet's soliloquy can be moving, but it does not hold a candle to seeing a great actor deliver the speech. When you get this chance to be a playwright, think about the ways that a theater performance is different from a book. What can you, as the writer, convey or express in a play that you could not in a book? Why do you think this is? What might the author of a novel be able to communicate that you as a playwright cannot? All forms of communication have their own advantages and drawbacks. Have fun exploring the ones that belong to theater.

Directions: Break into small groups of three or four people. Agree on a topic and write a short play together. (Try to be flexible; writing as a group can be very hard. Remember that you can write a play by yourself some other time if you feel like it.) After writing the play, put on all or part of your play for your classmates. Select someone from your group to direct the play, and the other group members will play the characters. Use the steps below to help you get started.

Title of Play

_____

_____

Main Characters

_____

_____

_____

Plot Summary

_____

_____

_____

_____

NCTE/IRA Standards
- 7, 11, 12

Time Required
- About two class periods

Teaching Tips

Students may work on the activity sheets individually, with a partner, or with a small group.

Activity Sheet 13A
- Help students connect the information about propaganda in ancient Sumer with their own experiences of propaganda.
- Teach students the term "stele."
- Emphasize the purpose of propaganda.

Activity Sheet 13B
- Make sure students understand why an argument with a logical fallacy is an incorrect argument.
- Help your students with the definitions provided.

Activity Sheet 13C
- Encourage students to analyze the propaganda they come across and evaluate it before making a decision.

Answers

- **Activity Sheet 13A** 1. Propaganda is an attempt to influence the attitudes of a community towards a specific position or belief; 2. The Sumerian List of Kings is almost 5,000 years old; 3. A stele is an upright column or pillar with inscriptions on it; 4. Answers will vary.
- **Activity Sheet 13B** Discuss with students.
- **Activity Sheet 13C** Answers will vary. Reward obvious effort and understanding of the fallacies.

Extension and Enrichment

- Students can watch current political commercials and advertisements and analyze them for logical fallacies in order to assess their validity.
- As a class experiment, have students write their own propaganda on a benign but obscure topic. Post the propaganda around the school and conduct surveys later to see if the propaganda worked.

Visit <u>WorldRecordsBooks.com</u> for more images and activities!

Name _____ Class _____ Date _____

Directions: Read the article and complete the activities.

For as long as people have been writing, people have been writing propaganda. *Propaganda* is any attempt to influence the attitude of a community towards a specific position or belief. Though this seems like a simple definition, in truth there are nearly 50 specific types of propaganda. The oldest propaganda found so far hails from ancient Sumer, the birthplace of writing. The Sumerian List of Kings, dating to 2900 BCE, lists all of the kings of Sumer and their accomplishments, both real and imagined. This list has also been found in conjunction with steles (large, upright stone pillars sporting written inscriptions) that depict images of kings slaying their enemies and leading armies.

It may surprise you to learn that most of the monuments left by ancient civilizations can be considered propaganda. From the famous pyramids to inscriptions on temple walls, to statues and steles—most were built solely to function as propaganda, proclaiming the might and achievements of rulers and nations.

Victory stele of Naram-Sin, a 23rd century BC Mesopotamian king.

1. What is propaganda?

_____

2. How old is the oldest extant propaganda in the world?

_____

3. What is stele?

_____

4. Are you aware of any modern propaganda similar to the propaganda of the ancient Sumerians?

_____

_____

In Eanna, Meskiaggasher, the son of (the sun god) Utu reigned as En (Priest) and Lugal (King) 324 years—Meskiaggasher entered the sea, ascended the mountains. Enmerkar, the son of Meskiaggasher, the king of erech who had built Erech, reigned 420 years as king. Lugalbanda, the shepherd, reigned 1,200 years. Dumuzi the fisherman, whose city was Kua, reigned 100 years.

— *from the Sumerian List of Kings*

Name _____ Class _____ Date _____

As you may have guessed from the fact that propaganda has been around as long as writing, the use of propaganda is a very common technique to influence people. Not only is it common, it's diverse, too. There are many different types of propaganda—as many as 50! That's a lot of ways to try to convince someone that you're right.

As you go about your daily life, you are constantly bombarded by propaganda, and you might not even realize it. As a responsible, free-thinking citizen, it's your job to decide what you will allow yourself to be influenced by. Some propaganda may be fair and even informative, but much of the propaganda we encounter is extremely biased and attempts to sway its audience without valid proof or evidence to support its claims.

Several types of propaganda are known as logical fallacies. A logical fallacy is a step in an argument which uses incorrect reasoning. Often, fallacies work to distract people from a lack of evidence or proof by introducing emotional or interpersonal influences. If propaganda contains one or more logical fallacies, then it is wise to think carefully about the point it is trying to make. Even if you decide that you believe what the propaganda is intended to convince you of, you should keep in mind that the argument being used is wrong and misleading.

1. Red Herring	This fallacy presents data or issues that are irrelevant to the argument at hand in order to distract from the topic.
2. Common Man	In this fallacy, the entity behind the propaganda attempts to sway people by acting like one of them and portraying their values.
3. Ad hominem	This is a direct personal attack against an opponent rather than against the opponent's arguments.
4. Ad nauseam	In this technique, an idea is repeated enough times that it begins to be taken as the truth. Usually the propagator controls the media.
5. Appeal to Authority	This fallacy cites popular or powerful figures who support an idea, issue, position, or course of action.
6. Appeal to Fear	Propaganda using an appeal to fear seeks to instill panic in the general population and offers the position it is designed to promote as the only safe course of action.
7. Bandwagon	This fallacy is an attempt to persuade the members of its audience that they must follow a particular course of action because other people are doing so.

Name _____ Class _____ Date _____

Directions: As you go about your day, pay careful attention to the advertisements you see and hear. Use the table below to record the propaganda and analyze it.

What was the propaganda advertising?	Type of media used (TV, radio, flyer, etc.)	Type of Propaganda

14. The World's First Printing Press

China in 1040 A.D. by Bi Sheng

NCTE/IRA Standards
• 4, 5, 12

Time Required
• About two class periods

Teaching Tips

• Students may work on the activity sheets individually, with a partner, or in small groups.

Activity Sheet 14A

• Emphasize that the printing press was first invented in Asia, but that Gutenberg later invented his independently.
• Explain how movable type was different and more effective than previous methods of printing.

Activity Sheet 14B

• Procure needed materials ahead of time. Note that you may want to spread coverings of some sort over the students' work areas to prevent stains from paint or ink. You may also wish to provide aprons for students or warn them ahead of time to wear old clothes.
• Encourage your students to try to replicate a selection of writing.

Activity Sheet 14C

• Help your students find historical resources to use in their essays.
• Review with your students how to research and write a paper using valid sources.

Answers

• *Activity Sheet 14A* 1. China; 1040 A.D.; 2. wooden ones; 3. 1440 CE; 4. Answers will vary. The printing press made the transmission of ideas and knowledge faster than ever before and, hence, facilitated many of the intellectual advances which have followed its invention.
• *Activity Sheet 14B* Results will vary. Reward genuine effort.
• *Activity Sheet 14C* Reward thoughtful and well-supported essays.

Extension and Enrichment

• To further reinforce the importance of printing, have students make a timeline of all the major revolutions of thought that happened before and after the invention of the printing press in Europe.

Visit WorldRecordsBooks.com for more images and activities!

Name _____ Class _____ Date _____

Directions: Read the article and complete the activities.

Many scholars agree that the single most important invention in the past millennium is the printing press. No other creation has sparked such a revolution in human thought and communication.

Though most Westerners believe that the first printing press was invented by Johannes Gutenberg around 1440 CE in Germany, the first printing press was actually invented in China around 1040 CE by the intellectual Bi Sheng. This press was the first to feature movable type and use wooden tiles with characters on them.

Over the next several hundred years, this design spread throughout Asia and was improved several times until metal movable type was invented in Korea around 1230 CE.

About 200 years later, Johannes Gutenberg independently invented his version of the movable type printing press. A goldsmith by trade, Gutenberg made substantial technological innovations which improved existing attempts at the printing press. One such invention was an alloy for the type that is still used today, and another is the hand mould, a method of casting the type pieces.

A Gutenberg Bible

Before the printing press was invented, it could take years to make a copy of a book. With Gutenberg's press, replicating a book took only days. Within less than a century, printed books were circulating around Europe and the rest of the world, bringing with them ideas and technology that would change the face of Western civilization forever.

1. In which country and year was the printing press invented?

_____

2. What kind of tiles did the first printing press use for the type?

_____

3. In what year did Johannes Gutenberg invent his version of the printing press?

_____

4. Why do you think the printing press is widely considered one of the greatest human inventions?

_____

Name _____ Class _____ Date _____

One of the greatest advantages to the printing press was that it allowed books to be printed exponentially faster than previous methods. Before the printing press, people wishing to make a copy of a book could either copy it by hand, like scribes, or they could use the wood block printing technique. Wood block printing was first used in Asia around 200 CE and in Egypt around 400 CE to print patterns onto textiles. Later, it was adapted to reproduce books and other written materials. To produce the wood block, the printer would cut the mirror image of the desired pattern or page onto a wooden block, dip it in ink or paint, and then press the block onto paper or cloth. As you might imagine, such a process took a long time. Books printed in that fashion could take years to complete. Nevertheless, block printing was the main method of writing reproduction for more than 1000 years. In fact, it is still preferred today by many artists and textile companies for its superior aesthetic quality.

Be a Block Printer!

Many artists today still use block printing to produce beautiful books and works of art. The process is very simple, though time consuming, and the results are well worth the effort. Here are the steps to make your own wood block prints.

Supplies:

- styrofoam sheets

- pens, pencils, and/or styli for etching

- ink or paint

- thick, absorbent paper such as newspaper, manila paper, or construction paper

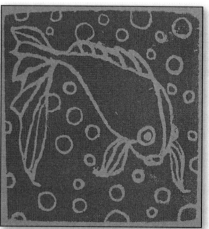

Directions:

1. Take appropriate precautions to protect your area from paint/ink stains. If needed, spread coverings over your work surface.

2. Using the writing tools, etch your picture into the styrofoam sheets, being careful not to poke all the way through. If you want to try your hand at printing something similar to a book, be sure to write all the letters backwards.

3. Dip the side of the styrofoam with your etchings on it into the paint or ink.

4. Carefully lift the styrofoam out of the paint or ink and press it wet-side down firmly and evenly onto a piece of paper.

5. Admire your artwork. You're a block printer!

Name _____ Class _____ Date _____

The printing press, though a marvelous technological innovation in itself, is important because of what it made possible. Once books could be rapidly reproduced, ideas and thoughts could be spread throughout the world at a faster pace than ever before. Gutenberg's printing press kicked off at least two revolutions within the first 100 years of its existence. Both were revolutions of thought. The first revolution was the Renaissance, a rebirth of art, science, and classical thinking that ultimately paved the way for the Enlightenment. The second revolution was the Protestant Reformation that swept Europe after Martin Luther posted his Ninety-Five Theses upon the doors of the Catholic Church (Castle Church in Wittenberg, Germany). The Ninety-Five Theses was almost immediately reprinted and sent to all corners of the continent, resulting in a monumental split in Christianity. Both of these events played vital roles in creating the world that we live in today. Without Gutenberg's printing press, who knows what life would be like?

Directions: Write an essay outlining another monumental event in history that would not have been possible without printing technology.

_____

_____

_____

_____

_____

_____

_____

_____

_____

_____

_____

_____

_____

15. The World's Most Popular Book
The Bible

NCTE/IRA Standards
- 3, 9, 11, 12

Time Required
- About two class periods

Teaching Tips

Students may work on the activity sheets individually, with a partner, or in small groups.

Activity Sheet 15A
- Emphasize that the Bible is also one of the world's oldest books.
- Inform students that Christianity is currently the world's most widely practiced religion.

Activity Sheet 15B
- It's easy to think of the downsides to only having one book. Encourage students to list as many benefits as they can.

Activity Sheet 15C
- Help students select passages appropriate for their skill levels and interests. You may also want to work with them on memorizing techniques.
- Encourage students to be word perfect.
- Have your students recite their passages in front of the class. Note that some will likely be more anxious about public speaking than others; be flexible and encouraging. You may wish to invite students to recite their passages privately for you.

Answers

- ***Activity Sheet 15A*** 1. No one has kept track of every book ever sold. It is thought that anywhere from 2.5 to 6 billion copies of the Bible have been sold since 1815; 2. 39 books; 66 books; 3. Answers will vary. Reward thoughtful responses; 4. Answers will vary. Reward thoughtful responses.
- ***Activity Sheet 15B*** Encourage creativity, but be sure students' responses make sense.
- ***Activity Sheet 15C*** Reward students for effort, accurate memorization, and good presentations.

Extension and Enrichment

- Students can conduct research on the sacred texts of other major religions and compare them with the Bible.

Visit <u>WorldRecordsBooks.com</u> for more images and activities!

Name _____ Class _____ Date _____

Directions: Read the article and complete the activities.

Though no one has kept track of the number of copies of every book ever sold, the book with the most estimated sales is the Bible, with anywhere from 2.5 to 6 billion copies sold worldwide since 1815.

The Bible is also one of the most influential books in the world. People have translated parts of the Bible into more than 2,000 different languages. This cannot be said of any other book. One of the main reasons for the Bible's popularity is that The Old Testament is one of the most sacred books for Christians and Jews. Jewish people recognize the books from Genesis to Malachi and base their faith and practices on these 39 books. Christians add 27 books to the Hebrew Bible to form the Christian Bible and incorporate the teachings of all 66 books into their faith. In addition to being the basis for two of the world's biggest faiths, the Bible has tremendous historical, literary, and philosophical value. It speaks in great detail about events from the ancient past and has exerted a great influence over many thinkers both modern and ancient; some of its teachings even form the basis for some governments' fundamental laws.

The Bible

1. Why can't we know exactly how many copies of the world's most popular book have been sold? What is the estimate?

_____

2. How many books are in the Hebrew Bible? How many are in the Christian Bible?

_____

3. Why do you think the Bible has been translated into more than 2,000 different languages?

_____

4. Do you think there is a connection between the Bible being the most sacred text for two of the world's major religions and it being the world's most popular book? Why or why not?

_____

Name _____ Class _____ Date _____

The Bible was often the only book that pioneers moving west across North America were able to take with them. Though most students today start off reading relatively short and simple books, in those days many children were taught to read using just the Bible.

Directions: Think about what it must have been like growing up with just one book. What would be the drawbacks to having only one book to read? What would be the benefits? Fill in the chart below with as many pros and cons as you can think of.

Benefits	Drawbacks

Name _____ Class _____ Date _____

One hundred and fifty years ago, an important part of school was memorization. Students memorized chapters and even whole books of the Bible—especially when that was the only book available. For long periods of history, the ability to quote passages from the Bible or other widely-recognized books was viewed as an important skill and the mark of an educated person. Have you ever memorized a chapter of a book?

Directions: Pick out one of your favorite books. From this book select a passage that you find particularly meaningful, insightful, or funny. Approve your selection with your teacher and then memorize that passage. Try to learn it well enough so that you will remember it years from now.

Favorite Book

Passage to Memorize

16. The World's Most Printed Poem

Ch'ang-sha

Teaching Tips

Students may work on the activity sheets individually, with a partner, or in small groups.

Activity Sheet 16A
- Explain the terms "Communism," "calligraphy," and "the People's Republic of China."
- Encourage students to do outside research to better understand Chinese history.

Activity Sheet 16B
- Teach students the basic literary elements provided.
- Help students to understand the difference between "metaphor" and "simile."

Activity Sheet 16C
- Help students choose appropriate types of poetry or poets to emulate. After they have chosen, help students identify distinctive features to imitate in their own poems.
- Encourage students not to be intimidated, and reward creativity.

Answers

- *Activity Sheet 16A* 1. more than 400 million copies; 2. 30 years; 3. Maoism, Communism; 4. China is the most populous country in the world, and Mao held an extremely powerful position there. The government he headed used censorship and propaganda as tools to further its political agenda, and thus, it is likely that many people had reason to read his work, whether because of personal interest or external pressure.
- *Activity Sheet 16B* Answers will vary but should demonstrate an understanding of the literary elements and the poem. 1. Possible answers include "thousand hills crimsoned through"; 2. Possible answers include "Pointing to our mountains and rivers/Setting people afire with our words"; 3. Possible answers include reflective, thoughtful; 4. Yes, "we struck the waters/and the waves stayed the speeding boats."; 5. Answers will vary. The translator needs to compensate for the differences in the languages.
- *Activity Sheet 16C* Reward honest effort.

Extension and Enrichment

- Have students research traditional forms of poetry used in other cultures and give presentations on their favorites.
- Organize a poetry slam for your class and encourage students to perform their own work.

Visit WorldRecordsBooks.com for more images and activities!

Name _____ Class _____ Date _____

Directions: Read the article and complete the activities.

Though many of the world's greatest poems were written by poets who devoted their lives to their art, the poem which has been printed the most times was written by a man who was extremely busy with other things. "Ch'ang-sha," a poem written by Chairman Mao Zedong, has sold more than 400 million copies since it was written in 1925—substantially more copies than any other poem ever written.

Chairman Mao was the leader of the People's Republic of China from its establishment in 1949 until his death in 1979. A skilled political philosopher, military strategist, public speaker, revolutionary, calligraphist, and poet, Mao was named by *Time Magazine* as one of the top 100 most important people of the century. He radically changed the face of Communism, and his own particular communist philosophy is now called Maoism. He is both hailed in China as the savior of the nation and, conversely, criticized for his political purges, which are believed to have caused the deaths of between 50 and 70 million people. In addition to his poetry, Mao wrote *Quotations from Chairman Mao*, a work which is second only to the Bible on the list of best-selling books.

Ch'ang-sha, a poem written by Chairman Mao Zedong.

1. How many copies of "Ch'ang-sha" have been sold?

_____

2. How long was Chairman Mao the leader of the People's Republic of China?

_____

3. What political philosophy is named after Mao? What is it an adaptation of?

_____

4. How might Mao's country of origin and political position have influenced the number of copies that have been sold of his poems and other works?

_____

Name _____ Class _____ Date _____

Poets employ many different tools in their craft. These tools are called literary elements, and they provide a framework for both creating and understanding written works. Some commonly used literary elements in poetry are alliteration, tone, irony, metaphor, simile, symbolism, meter, rhyme, image, and diction. Isolating and analyzing these elements can help readers to better understand and appreciate the work they are studying.

Directions: Read the poem below. Then answer the questions.

Ch'ang-sha — 1925, Mao Zedong

Alone I stand in the autumn cold
On the tip of Orange Island,
The Xiang flowing northward;
I see a thousand hills crimsoned through
By their serried woods deep-dyed,
And a hundred barges vying
Over crystal blue waters.
Eagles cleave the air,
Fish glide under the shallow water;
Under freezing skies a million creatures contend in freedom.
Brooding over this immensity,
I ask, on this bondless land
Who rules over man's destiny?

I was here with a throng of companions,
Vivid yet those crowded months and years.
Young we were, schoolmates,
At life's full flowering;
Filled with student enthusiasm
Boldly we cast all restraints aside.
Pointing to our mountains and rivers,
Setting people afire with our words,
We counted the mighty no more than muck.
Remember still
How, venturing midstream, we struck the waters
And the waves stayed the speeding boats?

1. Cite an example of imagery in this poem.

_____

_____

_____

2. How does Mao use symbolism in this poem?

_____

_____

_____

3. What is the tone of this poem?

_____

_____

_____

4. Does Mao use metaphor in this poem?

_____

_____

_____

5. This poem has been translated from its original Chinese into English. How do you think this might affect elements like diction, alliteration, meter, and rhyme?

_____

_____

_____

_____

_____

Name _____ Class _____ Date _____

Some of the oldest examples of writing have been found in poetry. People have been writing poetry for thousands of years, and now it is your turn.

Directions: There are many different types and styles of poetry. Some (such as sonnets) have rigid forms with particular rules about rhyme schemes and meter. Others' rules are much looser; it is debatable whether free verse has any. Poems also tackle a wide variety of subjects. Some tell stories, some tell jokes, others are philosophical or religious in nature, and some simply capture a moment or feeling. Use the Internet or any available books of poetry to look at examples of different poets' styles. Once you have seen a variety, choose a particular form of poetry to use or a particular poet to imitate. Relax, feel free to be playful, and try your hand at writing a poem in your chosen form or style about a topic of your choice.

_____

_____

_____

_____

_____

_____

_____

_____

_____

_____

_____

_____

_____

_____

NCTE/IRA Standards
- 1, 2, 6. 11, 12

Time Required
- About three class periods

Teaching Tips
Students may work on the activity sheets individually, with a partner, or in small groups.

Activity Sheet 17A
- Emphasize that different people have different preferences when it comes to books, and the satisfaction that each person gains from reading any given book can be relative.
- Remind students that books can be classified into different genres.

Activity Sheet 17B
- Encourage students to collaborate when identifying protagonists and antagonists.

Activity Sheet 17C
- Encourage students to be concise.
- Have students select the passages they like most.

Answers
- *Activity Sheet 17A* 1. Agatha Christie; 2. Mrs. Marple and Hercule Poirot; 3. Answers will vary. Reward thoughtful responses; 4. Answers will vary. Reward thoughtful responses.
- *Activity Sheet 17B* 1. G; 2. H; 3. A; 4. B; 5. C; 6. F; 7. E; 8. D.
  9-12. Encourage students to use protagonists and antagonists from books they have read.
- *Activity Sheet 17C* Reward clear, thoughtful reports.

Extension and Enrichment
- Students can read one of Agatha Christie's novels or short stories and think about what makes her works so popular.
- Students can write short detective stories of their own.

Visit WorldRecordsBooks.com for more images and activities!

The World's Bestselling Author

Activity Sheet 17A

Name _____ Class _____ Date _____

Directions: Read the article and complete the activities.

How many books do you have in your room? How about in your home? In your school? Not very many people have counted the number of books they have. It may surprise you to learn that until recently, many publishers didn't keep exact counts of how many books they had sold. Not knowing how many books have been sold makes it much harder to determine the world's best-selling author. Even though we lack exact figures, we do have good estimates for how many books have been sold by the world's most widely read authors. The world's best-selling author is almost definitely Agatha Christie. Somewhere between 2 and 4 million copies of her books have been sold. Shakespeare's plays have sold around the same number of copies. (As a playwright, Shakespeare was not considered for this world record).

Agatha Christie is best known for writing mystery novels. She helped define the genre that we know so well today. She wrote a grand total of 85 books. Her two most famous protagonists are Mrs. Marple and Hercule Poirot. A *protagonist* is the main character of a story, and often the person from whose point of view the story is told. While Mrs. Marple and Hercule Poirot never worked together, each of them faced many antagonists. An *antagonist* is the villain of a story.

Agatha Christie

1. Who is considered the world's best-selling author?

   _____

2. Who are the two most famous protagonists in her works?

   _____

3. Agatha Christie is reported to have grown very tired of one of her protagonists. Why do you think an author might grow weary of writing about one of her most popular characters?

   _____

4. What do you think people like about detective novels?

   _____

Name _____ Class _____ Date _____

People like reading about conflicts and difficult situations. Authors know this and often write about a struggle between a few well-drawn characters.

Directions: The lists below contain some famous protagonists and antagonists from a number of literary works. Match each protagonist on the left with his or her antagonist on the right. Fill in the last three rows with three pairs of protagonists and antagonists from books of your own choice.

Protagonists	Antagonists
1. Sherlock Holmes	A. Cardinal Richelieu
2. Harry Potter	B. Mr. Hyde
3. The Three Musketeers	C. Sauron
4. Dr. Jekyll	D. Captain Hook
5. Frodo Baggins	E. Queen of Hearts
6. Dorothy	F. Wicked Witch of the West
7. Alice	G. Professor Moriarty
8. Peter Pan	H. Lord Voldemort
9.	I.
10.	J.
11.	K.
12.	L.

Literary Criticism: A Book Report

Activity Sheet 17C

Name _____ Class _____ Date _____

What does a critic do? Perhaps because the word "critic" comes from the same root as the word "criticism," it sometimes seems as though critics spend most of their time disparaging that which they critique. But in actuality, it is the job of a literary critic to think deeply about what he or she reads. Be a literary critic. Why do you think Agatha Christie's books have been so popular? Or, to put it another way, what makes a good book a good book?

Directions: Reread a favorite book. This time though, look for the things that you really like in the novel, and write them down. Are there lots of funny moments or lines? Do the characters seem real? Do the descriptions let you visualize new or exciting places? Think about what you like in the book. When you are done, write a three-page book report.

Chosen Book

Things I Like About this Book

NCTE/IRA Standards
• 7, 8, 11, 12

Time Required
• About four class periods

Teaching Tips

Students may work on the activity sheets individually, with a partner, or in small groups. Activity Sheet 18B is designed for students to complete individually or in pairs, though the number of students in your class may necessitate larger groups.

Activity Sheet 18A
• Make sure students understand the terms "Islam," "Fatwa," and "Supreme Leader of Iran."
• Help students understand why many Muslims are offended by Rushdie's depictions of the Prophet.

Activity Sheet 18B
• Explain the meaning of the terms 'libel' and 'slander.'
• Divide the topics among the students and help them conduct research.
• Help students focus on what their topics reveal about free speech in America.
• Encourage the class to make connections between the information presented in different students' reports.

Activity Sheet 18C
• Ensure that your students know how to write a persuasive essay.

Answers

• *Activity Sheet 18A* 1. Governments censor media to suppress information they deem inconvenient, offensive, or inappropriate; 2. *The Satanic Verses* is banned in many Islamic countries because the depictions of the Prophet Muhammad are judged by Islamic authorities to be blasphemous; 3. Answers will vary. Reward thoughtful responses.
• *Activity Sheet 18B* Reward good research and informative presentations.
• *Activity Sheet 18C* Reward essays that are well-developed and thoroughly address the prompt.

Extension and Enrichment

• Organize a debate in which your students defend or protest the banning of a book.
• Have your class host its own Banned Books Week.

Visit WorldRecordsBooks.com for more images and activities!

Name _____ Class _____ Date _____

Censorship is the suppression or erasure of material which someone with power deems harmful, inappropriate, or inconvenient. All sorts of media may be subject to censorship. Today this includes a wide variety of content transmitted by modern technology; in China, for example, the government has taken measures to prevent its citizens from having access to certain web sites. Traditionally, however, the object of censorship has mostly been writings.

Hundreds of books have been banned somewhere in the world, including many which we now consider great literature. Over time, many countries have become more tolerant of books expressing potentially uncomfortable views, and most are now much more relaxed about what literature can be published and sold within their borders. Nevertheless, certain books offend certain governments so much that censorship of written works is still very much present in the world today.

Salman Rushdie

The Satanic Verses by Salman Rushdie is one such work. Banned in more than 15 Islamic countries for its unflattering portrayal of the Prophet Muhammad, it is likely the world's most controversial book. When *The Satanic Verses* was first released in 1989, there were riots in Pakistan and several people were killed. That February, the Ayatollah Khomeini, Supreme Leader of Iran, issued a fatwa calling on all Muslims to kill or help kill the book's author and its publishers. Since then, 38 people have died during attempts on the lives of Rushdie and others connected with the book. Rushdie remains unharmed mostly due to the extensive police protection he has been afforded since his novel was first published.

1. Why do governments censor media?

_____

2. Why is *The Satanic Verses* banned in so many countries?

_____

3. What do you think? Should governments have the right to suppress material they find inconvenient or inappropriate? Explain why or why not.

_____

_____

Name _____ Class _____ Date _____

In the United States, we have many freedoms that are guaranteed to us by our Constitution and the Bill of Rights. Some of the most important are found in the First Amendment, which was originally written only to apply to Congress, but which has since been interpreted by the Supreme Court (using the Fourteenth Amendment) as applying to all levels of government. The First Amendment reads as follows:

Congress shall make no law respecting an establishment of religion, or prohibiting the free exercise thereof; or abridging the freedom of speech, or of the press; or the right of the people peaceably to assemble, and to petition the Government for a redress of grievances.

As you can see, one right that the First Amendment protects is freedom of speech. This is the right which prevents controversial books such as *The Satanic Verses* from being banned by the government in America. In general, freedom of speech means that citizens in America are guaranteed the opportunity to express their thoughts and opinions without fear of government authorities punishing them for doing so. Such a right is extremely important in a free society, where the government is supposed to answer to its people and where citizens need open discussion and accurate information in order to be informed voters.

Though freedom of speech is vital to a healthy democracy, there are many issues that arise when putting it into practice. In other words, our freedom of expression as citizens is not absolute. For example, libel, slander, certain forms of obscenity, and certain types of speech which are judged to pose a threat to the nation are illegal in the United States. Many issues concerning freedom of speech remain controversial. Courts have struggled over the years to balance individual liberties with societal welfare and to define what actions constitute "speech."

Directions: Choose one of the following topics. Working individually or with a partner, research your topic, focusing on what the event, controversy, or ruling reveals about free speech in America. Try to understand each side of the issues involved, and write up a brief report of your findings.

- The Sedition Act of 1798 (one of the Alien and Sedition Acts)

- The Espionage Act of 1917

- The Sedition Act of 1918

- The Pentagon Papers

- *National Socialist Party of America* v. *Village of Skokie* (Supreme Court Case)

- *Texas* v. *Johnson* (Supreme Court case)

- *1989 Flag Protection Act and United States* v. *Eichman* (Supreme Court case)

- The Smith Act of 1940

- *Tinker* v. *Des Moines* (Supreme Court case)

- *Feiner* v. *New York* (Supreme Court case)

- *New York Times Co.* v. *Sullivan* (Supreme Court case)

- *Citizens United* v. *Federal Election Commission* (Supreme Court case)

- *Virginia* v. *Black* (Supreme Court case)

- The Patriot Act

_____

_____

_____

_____

_____

_____

_____

_____

_____

_____

_____

_____

_____

_____

Name _____ Class _____ Date _____

School libraries are not forbidden by the First Amendment to decide which books to provide for students. However, the Supreme Court ruled in *Board of Education, Island Trees School District v. Pico* that there are some restrictions on which books a school library can choose to remove from its collection.

Directions: Are there any circumstances under which you think it would be acceptable or even good to ban a book from a school library? Try to think about possible arguments both for and against such an action before you make up your mind. Write a persuasive essay supporting your viewpoint.

_____

_____

_____

_____

_____

_____

_____

_____

_____

_____

_____

_____

_____

_____

_____

_____

_____

NCTE/IRA Standards
• 7, 8, 12

Time Required
• About three class periods

Teaching Tips
Students may work on the activity sheets individually, with a partner, or in small groups. The last activity sheet calls for a race, so each student should get one question from the list to answer.

Activity Sheet 19A
• Point out the importance of having all of these materials organized and safely stored.
• Explain the roles of legislators and Supreme Court justices and why they have special library privileges.

Activity Sheet 19B
• Show students where Alexandria is on a map. Try to incorporate pictures and other resources.
• Make a brief timeline of Egyptian history spanning the relevant era.

Activity Sheet 19C
• Before setting the students loose, lead a demonstration or have a librarian demonstrate how to use the catalogue system to find materials in the library.
• Help the class divide the questions amongst themselves. Students may work alone, but the exercise will probably be more fun if they work in teams, with each team trying to answer its questions before the other teams answers theirs.

Answers
• **Activity Sheet 19A** 1. the Library of Congress; 2. 141,847,810 items; 3. Answers will vary. Reward thoughtful responses; 4. Encourage student browsing.
• **Activity Sheet 19B** Reward thoughtful answers written with care. Preservation of knowledge is important to all peoples in all times. The Library of Alexandria was a cultural treasure.
• **Activity Sheet 19C** Results will vary. The importance is in the research skills acquired.

Extension and Enrichment
• For more practice using the library, students can give presentations on various topics using only information found in the library.
• Students can conduct further research on the greatest libraries in the world and how they have compared to one another.

Visit WorldRecordsBooks.com for more images and activities!

The World's Largest Library

Activity Sheet 19A

Name _____ Class _____ Date _____

Directions: Read the article and complete the activities.

Libraries are wonderful places. Their books serve as repositories of cultural knowledge and gateways to millions of different adventures and experiences. Though the Internet has made a lot of information accessible to the public that was formerly only available in libraries, these houses of books remain places of scholarship and inquiry.

There is no limit, large or small, to what constitutes a library. If you have even a few books on a shelf in your room, then that is your personal library. On the other end of the spectrum, national libraries may contain millions of books in multiple buildings.

The world's largest library is the United States Library of Congress, located in Washington D.C.. Founded in 1800, the Library of Congress resides in three large buildings and currently houses 141,847,810 items, including books, periodicals, music,

monographs, serials, and other items. The Library receives copies of every map, book, musical composition, pamphlet, and print registered in the United States—everything that has ever been published in the U.S. is available there! Though the Library is open to visitors, only legislators, Supreme Court justices, high-ranking government officials, and some of these persons' staffs are allowed to check out books. The Library staff's largest duty is to conduct research in response to Congressional inquiries regarding topics of interest to the legislative branch.

The Library of Congress

1. What is the world's largest library?

_____

2. How many catalogued materials does the library hold?

_____

3. Why do you think only certain people are allowed to take books out of the Library?

_____

4. Visit www.loc.gov. Write a brief paper about what you find.

Name _____ Class _____ Date _____

Directions: Read the article and then answer the questions.

History is full of references to lost wonders of Western civilization: the lost continent of Atlantis, the Colossus of Rhodes, the Hanging Gardens of Babylon. However, few such wonders are lamented so bitterly as the lost Royal Library of Alexandria.

The Library of Alexandria was constructed in 300 BCE in Egypt and was the greatest library in the ancient world. Though no index of its collections exists today, scholars estimate that at one time the library held several hundred thousand scrolls. Apocryphal sources claim that librarians were able to acquire so many scrolls because laws required all citizens and any ships that entered port to surrender anything with writing on it to the library scribes, who would then make copies for the library. In addition, the library enjoyed the patronage of the Ptolemy family, the rulers of Egypt. This meant that the library had a nearly limitless budget for book acquisition and was able to support an army of scholars and scribes in passionate pursuit of cataloging all human knowledge.

Unfortunately, the Royal Library of Alexandria no longer exists. Scholars believe that over a period of several centuries multiple fires and the wrath of the Catholic Church lead to the complete destruction of the library somewhere around 400 CE. The knowledge contained in the scrolls at Alexandria is thought to have been of incredible breadth, and scholars around the world have lamented its loss ever since the library's ruin.

Artist's rendition of the ancient Library of Alexandria.

Why might the acquisition and preservation of knowledge have been so important to the ancients? Why do you think the loss of the Library of Alexandria is still lamented today?

_____

_____

_____

_____

_____

Name _____ Class _____ Date _____

Many people now consider libraries to be obsolete since some of the information they contain can be found much more quickly online. Nevertheless, libraries are still the best source of information for many types of research that require depth as well as breadth in their source material. Though hundreds of pages on a certain topic may be available online, information gleaned from the internet is often merely topical, providing only introductory material on a given subject. For serious, in-depth research, a good library will almost always be the better choice.

Directions: Divide the following questions randomly. Grab a stopwatch and head to the library. Using ONLY the library catalogue, a librarian, the books in the library, and your own critical thinking skills, answer the first ten questions below. Then answer the second ten questions using the Internet. What can you conclude?

1. What was the population of Canada in 1989?

2. On what continent is Juu spoken?

3. What was the currency in Greece before the euro?

4. What was the GDP of Argentina in 2002?

5. How many breeds of horses are there in the world?

6. What is the tallest mountain in the world? How tall is it?

7. How many people speak English in the world?

8. In what country is the religion of Santeria practiced?

9. What is the tallest Mayan pyramid?

10. What is the Mandarin word for "brother"?

11. When was the first airplane built?

12. In what city was Leonardo da Vinci born?

13. How many plays did Shakespeare write?

14. What is the capitol of Croatia?

15. How many states are there in India?

16. What is the official religion of Egypt?

17. Where were the oldest human fossils found? How old are they?

18. Are Geraniums perennial or annual flowers?

19. What plant did aspirin originally come from?

20. How old is the Ramayana?

20. The World's First Screenplay
Cendrillon

NCTE/IRA Standards
• 3, 5, 11, 12

Time Required
• About three class periods

Teaching Tips

The activity sheets can be completed by students working independently, with partners, or in small groups.

Activity Sheet 20A
• Emphasize that screenplays are some of the most recent additions to literature.
• Encourage students to watch some early films to grow accustomed to the differences between modern and older movies.

Activity Sheet 20B
• Encourage students to think in terms of the similarities between story structures.
• Ask students what kinds of similar characters appear in their stories.

Activity Sheet 20C
• Be sure to approve selected films.
• Many critics consider *Jaws* to be one of the few movies better than the book on which it is based.

Answers

• *Activity Sheet 20A* 1. Since 1879; 2. the world's first projected films were scenes from everyday life; 3. Answers will vary. Reward thoughtful responses.

• *Activity Sheet 20B* Encourage students to discuss the shape of the narratives they most recently encountered. If time allows, discuss as a class stories the students have found predictable and why.

• *Activity Sheet 20C* Reward clear and well thought-out answers.

Extension and Enrichment

• Students can examine Méliès's most famous film, *Le Voyage dans la Lune*. Students can write a report evaluating which aspects of *Le Voyage dans la Lune* are depicted in modern movies.
• Students can create their own short films demonstrating the narrative structure outlined by Freytag.

Visit WorldRecordsBooks.com for more images and activities!

Name _____ Class _____ Date _____

Directions: Read the article and complete the activities.

A *screenplay* is a play meant to be seen either in a movie form or on television. In order to determine the world's first screenplay, we have to figure out what the world's first movie was. The first motion picture was visible through a slit in a device called a "zoopraxiscope." In 1879, the moving images displayed on a zoopraxiscope lasted for a few seconds and were hand-drawn. Next, in 1894, Thomas Edison's "Kinetoscope" let one person at a time look at moving images of real life. Then in 1895, Louis Lumière invented the "cinématographe", which was one of the first devices to be able to project moving images so multiple people could watch at once.

The first films to be presented to the public were of everyday events—people leaving a factory, a baby's breakfast, and swimming in the ocean, to name a few. These films were different from the movies we watch today. There was no script, no plot, and no story. These realistic films were the precursors of modern day documentaries.

It wasn't until Georges Méliès arrived on the scene that everything began to change. Méliès thought that films should be like the theater, a means to escape from reality. As a magician and illusionist, his first films demonstrated some of the earliest special effects, such as "The Disappearing Woman." Shortly thereafter, Méliès broke into the world of narrative film, and the world's first movie was born.

In 1899, *Cendrillon* hit the big screen. You might recognize it better by the name *Cinderella*. Méliès took a familiar story and showed it to the world in a new way. That means *Cendrillon* also carries the title of world's first screenplay.

Gustave Doré's illustration for Cendrillon

1. How long have motion pictures existed?

_____

2. What was the subject matter of the world's first projected films?

_____

3. Why do you think Méliès chose a fairy tale as his first narrative film?

_____

Name _____ Class _____ Date _____

When you watch a movie or read a book, do you ever feel like you can predict what will happen next? How do you feel when you were exactly right? The first time, it is probably a really good feeling, but if that happens too much, you will probably get bored. How do you know what will happen next? Even if you don't think about it, you know what shape a story is supposed to take.

The *plot* is all the events of a story that take place in it. Plots frequently take the following shape: introduction ➜ rising action ➜ climax ➜ falling action ➜ conclusion. Gustav Freytag, a German novelist and playwright, developed this layout of a plot. In the introduction, we get to know the characters and what's going on. In the rising action, a conflict or problem comes up, which builds to the climax. The climax is the peak of a story. What the ending is like is determined by how the climax unfolds. After the climax, the falling action is when the story winds down to the conclusion, where the story finishes.

Directions: Track the plot of the two most recent works of fiction you have read. After you finish, gather into a small group and compare with your classmates. How many of your stories fit this plot outline? For the ones that didn't fit, talk about how they were different.

INTRODUCTION	
RISING ACTION	
CLIMAX	
FALLING ACTION	
CONCLUSION	

INTRODUCTION	
RISING ACTION	
CLIMAX	
FALLING ACTION	
CONCLUSION	

Name _____ Class _____ Date _____

A great many movies are based on books. Since we imagine characters and settings as we read, seeing the movie based on a favorite book is often disappointing. "I liked the book better" is a common refrain.

Still, many movies based on books are excellent (and a handful are even better than the book!).

Directions: Choose one or more of the titles in the box. Read the book on which it is based, and then watch the movie. Then write an essay that answers these questions: Which did you like better, the book or the movie? Why?

Famous Movies Based on Books

- 2001: A Space Odyssey
- Apollo 13
- Babe
- The Bridge on the River Kwai
- A Beautiful Mind
- Casino Royale
- Charlotte's Web
- The Chronicles of Narnia: The Lion, the Witch and the Wardrobe
- Dances With Wolves
- Die Hard
- Field of Dreams
- Forrest Gump
- Friday Night Lights
- Fried Green Tomatoes
- Harry Potter and the Chamber of Secrets
- Harry Potter and the Deathly Hallows
- Harry Potter and the Goblet of Fire
- Harry Potter and the Half-Blood Prince
- Harry Potter and the Order of the Phoenix
- Harry Potter and the Philosopher's Stone
- Harry Potter and the Prisoner of Azkaban
- The Hunt for Red October

- Jaws
- The Last of the Mohicans
- Lord of the Flies
- The Lord of the Rings: The Fellowship of The Ring
- The Lord of the Rings: The Return of the King
- The Lord of the Rings: The Two Towers
- Master and Commander: The Far Side of the World
- Of Mice and Men
- The Natural
- Planet of the Apes
- Pride and Prejudice
- The Princess Bride
- Quiz Show
- Raging Bull
- A River Runs Through It
- Romancing the Stone
- The Untouchables
- The Verdict
- Willy Wonka and the Chocolate Factory
- Wuthering Heights

Made in the USA
San Bernardino, CA
13 April 2017